DO OR DIE

How I Escaped Life with a Murderer

How I Escaped Life with a Murderer

RITA HARLING

This edition published in 2011 by
Y Books
Lucan, Co. Dublin, Ireland
Tel / fax: +353 1 6217992
publishing@ybooks.ie
www.ybooks.ie

Paperback	ISBN: 978-1-908023-12-4
Ebook – Mobi format	ISBN: 978-1-908023-13-1
Ebook – epub format	ISBN: 978-1-908023-14-8

A CIP catalogue record for this book is available from the British Library.

Publisher's note: Some names have been changed to protect the identities of individuals.

10 9 8 7 6 5 4 3 2 1

Typeset by Y Books
Cover design by Graham Thew Design
Front cover images courtesy of iStock
Back cover photo courtesy of Peter Evers Photography
Printed and bound by Cox & Wyman, Reading, England

Dedication

I am dedicating this book to the memory of another mum of two who found herself in a similar situation to mine.
To Baiba Saulite, whose life ended too soon.
May she rest in peace.

Also to the memory of my dear parents,
Bridget and Nicholas Harling.

Acknowledgements

I would like to thank three people that have made the publication of this book possible. Without their professionalism I could not have done it. Thank you to Chenile Keogh, Managing Director and Publisher of Y Books, who has had faith in me from the very beginning and has also given unending encouragement. To Robert Doran, Publishing Manager of Y Books for his positive attitude and direction. I would also like to say a huge thank you to my editor, Síne Quinn, for her patience and guidance – your help is greatly appreciated. I have enjoyed working with all of you and I wish you every success in your future projects. Thank you all for helping me realise my dream and for helping me to move away from the past towards a brighter future.

Thank you to my sister, Mary, and my brother, Joe, for their great support. Thank you also to my nieces, Hazel and Emma, and my nephew, David.

Thank you to my children, Robyn and Conor. Without them in my life, I do not think that I could have carried on.

A special thanks to Tony for his love, support and understanding.

A big thank you to the many friends who stood by me and never judged me.

Table of Contents

Introduction

Today I watched a father grasp his son's hand as the child took what seemed to be his first steps. The child must have been about a year old. I sat in the car and watched as I waited for my son Conor to come out of school. The touching scene brought me back to my younger years and made me think about the short time that I had spent with my own father, who I had loved so dearly. How I have wished that my father was still a part of my life today. If he was still around maybe everything would have turned out differently. Maybe I would have gained from his wisdom and unconditional love. Sadly, my dad passed away when I was just ten years old; heart disease was a main contributor to his death. I have always missed him and have probably spent most of my adult life in search of him. I have had my regrets, but then who doesn't? However, I do have one serious regret, and that is to have ever laid eyes on Brian Kenny on that faithful day on which we met in 1995. I can honestly say that he ruined my life and the lives of many other people who fell victim to his ruthless, evil and twisted mind.

In October 2008 crime writer Paul Williams' book

Crime Wars was published. The book was a compilation of stories told by victims of organised crime in Dublin, Limerick and various cities in Europe. I was aware of the book's publication, but I did not rush out to buy it. Although I was suspicious that the past would never remain quiet and I was aware that something was bound to remind me of the horrific nightmare that was once my life, I didn't expect the book to unearth the horrid memories that I had so badly tried to bury and forget. At the time I was focused on trying to continue with my life and raise my kids out of harm's way. I will never forget the feeling of nausea I felt when my eighteen-year-old daughter came home and broke the news that my name had been published in Paul Williams' latest book. I had been successfully trying to move on with my life and not give Brian Kenny any more thought or energy. I had moved on for my children's sake and for the sake of my own sanity.

I was in shock: no one had contacted me to inform me that my name would be printed or to request my permission. I don't think anyone really knew how I felt about this. I do not believe that the author really cared, especially since he would not be the one who would be afraid to go to work. He wouldn't feel humiliated that his past was printed and that his private life was in the public domain. Although I believe it is right for the truth to be told, some people pay a higher price than others.

I did not go back to work after the book was published, and I began to worry about my future. I had worked in the travel industry for the previous ten years, and I had loved every minute of my career. I had been working for a major airline for the previous four years, as a reservations agent. I enjoyed working with the people there, and always kept my past firmly in the past in an effort to protect my kids' futures. I kept a roof over our heads and food on the table. I couldn't go to work that week because I felt that the office would be filled with Chinese whispers. The thought of everyone in work knowing that I was Brian Kenny's partner made me sick. I couldn't face any more humiliation. I was humiliated when I was with Brian Kenny and then I was humiliated by being associated with him – even if it was over ten years ago. To this day even the very mention of his name makes me want to vomit.

I have tried to maintain my privacy. I have hidden the truth from people who I have met and worked with. I have rarely opened up and have not spoken about the experiences that I suffered living at the mercy of Brian

Kenny. I was ashamed. I was ashamed of what people would think of me, of the assumptions they would make – guilty by association, as they say …

2008 was a bad year for me. As well as dealing with the release of the book, I was grieving for my mother. My mam passed away that December. She was a brave woman and was not afraid to stand up to Brian. His threats to her in the past did not faze her. Throughout my ordeal, she stood strong beside me. How I miss her.

It is because of these events that I now feel that I want to tell my story. Although I know that it will not change the past hurt that I endured, I hope it might help someone in a similar situation to mine – someone who feels scared and vulnerable and is not sure how to escape a difficult and frightening situation.

Chapter One

Happier Times

Before I met Brian Kenny, I had a relatively colourful, safe and moderate life. I was happy growing up. My mam did her utmost for us. When I look back and think of the happy memories I had, it is hard to understand how things turned out the way they did.

It was Christmas 1976 and our father had passed away that May. That year Mam bought my brother Joe and me new bicycles, both of them Eskas. Joe's was gold and mine was bright red. We were delighted to see our new bikes. We would never have considered at the time where the money came from; we were too young. Mam had in fact taken out a Credit Union loan. It was Dad's last request before he died that we would get new bikes, as he had been so protective of us and we had not been allowed to have them. It was a request that Mam saw through. I remember Joe and I hauling the bikes upstairs on Christmas Eve, just so we could wake up to see them on Christmas morning. It was probably about five in the morning when we woke up and tried to get the bikes back down the stairs. Joe was the bossy one. He wanted his downstairs first. I don't know where he thought he was going at five in the morning. Joe straddled the bike at the top of the stairs and I held on to the carrier as he tried to guide it down the stairs while holding on to the banister. He protested, telling me that I was holding him back. He told me to let go, which I did. With that Joe went down the stairs like a rocket, crashing into the glass table at the bottom of the stairs. Mam was awoken by all the drama and the mess was soon cleaned up. I still laugh about that today – the sight of Joe cycling out of control down the stairs. It was so funny.

Dad was very protective of us. He always made sure that we were held correctly as babies, making sure that the sun was not in our eyes. He did not like letting us out to play in the snow for fear of us getting colds. Although I remember on one occasion we made a huge snowman in the front garden with him. He was such a loving father. He was a hard worker. He worked on the CIE road freight. He would deliver cargo to every county in Ireland, north and south. He believed that weekends were our mother's break time. So, he always took us out for the day on Saturdays. We either went to the cinema or the zoo, and always to mass in the Pro-cathedral Church in the city centre. I also remember spending some afternoons in an Irish-speaking pub in town. I still have the shiny gold purse that he bought me in Hector Grey's one year. I always put it on the Christmas tree. If it was summer-time we would spend our time on Portmarnock beach. I remember the three of us digging holes in the sand. Dad would bury bottles of Fanta Lemon in the moist sand to keep them cool while we went swimming. We could never find the bottles of Fanta when we came back from our dip.

Our Dad was a brilliant swimmer. If you took your eyes off him for a second as he swam, you would not be able to find him again until his head popped up above the water at the other end of the beach. He was like a fish. I loved those days and the time that we spent with our father.

I can still nearly taste the Pink Elephant ice lollies that he would buy us on the way home. The odd weekend that we did not spend with him because of bad weather or because his work shifts changed, he never forgot us. He would arrive home with bags of Double Centre sweets and a half dozen bottles of Snowballs. We were allowed to share one, the rest were Mam's. I also remember him waking us up when he got home from work late. He always had something for us that the other kids on the road didn't have, like giant bubble gums or different types of sweets. Dad loved to try new things and new foods. I remember having spaghetti bolognese as a child and I also remember eating caviar. I loved caviar so much that I used to sneak into the kitchen and pick from the small jars that were in the fridge. I loved it, but I never understood what it was. If I was given it today there isn't a hope that I would eat it.

It is amazing what we take for granted today. I remember my mam ripening green bananas on the jacket-lagged boiler. Different fruits were a rarity thirty years ago. People forget things like that. They take things for granted nowadays. When we didn't know what existed out there we didn't need it.

We always holidayed in Wexford or in the UK. After our father's death, Mam always brought us away to Butlin's holiday camps. Every year we went to either Clacton-on-Sea in Essex or Pwehelli in Wales. Even with our father absent, we still had great childhoods. As there was only a year between Joe and me, we got on well most of the time. We could pal around together trying out most of the activities that the camp had to offer. I remember Joe winning the donkey derby one year; the prize was a free week at one of their sister camps, which Mam availed of the following year. I fell off my donkey as the bridle was not on right and no one noticed until I was half way around the racecourse and desperately trying to hold on. I was disgusted but Joe loved to jeer me over it later, boasting about winning his rosette and cup. Mam made sure that we had a holiday each year and she always thanked God for the Credit Union.

My sister Mary, who was a few years older than us, was married to David. They had married young and had two beautiful children at that stage, Hazel and D (David Jnr). Their third child, Emma, was born a number of years later. Every year the seven of us would travel to Butlin's. We loved it. Mam always took part in the glamorous grandmother competitions – she came second one year. David and David Jnr won the father and son competition. Mam won the Miss Personality competition. It was funny when they made her run around to the theme music from *The Benny Hill Show*. I will always have wonderful memories of those times.

Chapter Two

The Beginning

Brian Kenny was very charming when we met. He knew exactly how to gain my trust and friendship. He was also good to my daughter, which for me as a single parent was extremely important. I didn't know then that beneath this charming exterior lurked an evil and twisted sociopath. I am lucky that I am still here today. I'm lucky that I found my inner strength and escaped with my life. In every situation, however traumatic and terrifying, there is a way out, but it must be planned carefully. So many women have been murdered by their partners. So many women remain in violent relationships because they are afraid to leave. I understand exactly what that feels like. These manipulative brutes make it so hard for their victims; they threaten their children and their family members. It's more difficult because you have witnessed first-hand his capability of carrying through the threats and you stay in order to protect your family from the things he says he will do to them. Against your better judgement, you stay so that your family remains safe.

I carried on living with Brian Kenny for that reason, because of the threats that he made concerning my family members. He threatened to burn my mam's house to the ground while she slept. I had witnessed his sick mind in action, his cruel words, his powerful punches and his sheer disrespect for life. He was capable of following his threats through. I knew that, and time proved it when both Brian and Thomas Hinchon were convicted of the murder of Jonathan O'Reilly, who died on 17 April 2004. On 5 July 2005 Mr Justice Peart sentenced Brian Kenny and Thomas Hinchon to life for the murder.

Over time, Brian Kenny masterminded his little empire and eventually lost all reason, and as a result he is now serving time behind bars. After all the hurt that he had caused my family, he had finally made his own destiny: Mountjoy Prison.

ଡ ଓ

I first met Brian back in 1995. We had crossed paths on a few occasions while out with friends in Dublin's city centre. Though we knew each other to see, we never spoke to one another and I was not interested in him. I later learned that his grandmother lived around the corner from my mam's house. I knew his grandmother quite well and she was well respected in the community. I remember passing her house one day with my friend Martina; Brian was at her door. He shouted over and waved, I did not recognise him then and I asked Martina who he was. She told me that he had lived with his grandmother for a short period, as he had fallen out with his father. I had never seen him around the area before, and I never made the connection between him and the guy that we had met in town, until Martina told me who he was.

Months passed and I worked away as usual, plodding through life with relative ease. At that time I was happy, though at times it was hard work juggling parenting and a job. I worked at the Esso garage on the Finglas Road, beside Glasnevin Cemetery. I had worked there before the birth of my daughter Robyn. When Robyn was born I stopped working so I could mind her. At the time, I was living in a flat in Ballymun with her dad. We were happy for a while but then the relationship broke down. After things hadn't been going well for a while, we separated amicably. We had both played a part in the break-up of the relationship. Robyn's dad was not a bad man. He had never raised his voice nor laid a hand on me. I had found it hard to settle down and commit as I had been such a free spirit before. I was feeling trapped, and I believe that I may have been suffering from a mild form of post-natal depression. The relationship just was not working.

I went back to work in the Esso garage and continued to enjoy working there. After being away from home for a while and finding my independence, I decided that I would not go back and live with my mam. I decided to get a flat for myself and Robyn. We moved into a flat on Balbutcher Lane in Ballymun. It was on the same street as the flat that I had shared with Robyn's dad. Though it was hard being a working single parent, Robyn and I were happy and I enjoyed the time we had together. She was still seeing her father regularly before he moved to Europe. My mam helped me as much as she could, and my sister and her daughters also minded Robyn a lot. It was a long distance to commute every day. I would often have to get the bus to Finglas Village and walk the rest of the way up McKee Avenue to get to mam's, and then leave Robyn with her and get another bus to work.

One day I decided that I'd visit mam on my day off. It was a beautiful May day. We had planned a shopping trip and we were looking forward to it. Robyn and I were waiting for the bus right outside the block of flats on Balbutcher Lane in Ballymun. Robyn was a very cute and pretty kid, and we were looking well, decked out in our finery. We waited and waited but there was no sign of a bus. We were standing there for over an hour and I was getting agitated. It was then that I saw a red pick-up van indicate and pull in to the kerb in front of us. I had no idea who the driver was but I could tell that it was a man. He was wearing enormous sunglasses that hid his face. He rolled down the window and leaned forward so that I could see better. Then I realised who he was. It was Brian Kenny.

'Are you going to your mam's?' he asked.

'Eh, yeah,' I answered back, slightly embarrassed.

'Hop in! I'll give you a lift, I'm going to my gran's,' he offered.

I was glad to get the lift. We were both getting tired and it was becoming very hot. When we got into the van, Brian was really friendly and polite, much more than I had expected. He played and joked with Robyn as we drove to Finglas, and she really took a shine to him. When we eventually got to mam's, he reached over to the glove compartment and took out a notepad and pen. He scribbled down his phone number and handed it to me.

'Give me a ring if you fancy going for a drink sometime,' he said

I remember my face going bright red, and how I jumped out of the van as quick as I could. We waved him off and I glanced down at the piece of paper in my hand with his phone number on it. I shoved it deep down into the pocket of my jeans. I decided that I was going to take him up on his offer. Now I wonder, *why didn't that bus come?* It would have saved me years of hell! I didn't know it then, but I was about to make one of the worst decisions of my life by meeting Brian Kenny for a drink.

Over the coming months we started to go out and we were getting on really well. The relationship was becoming very serious. We did all the normal things couples in a new relationship do: go out for dinner, meet friends for drinks in town and occasionally we went clubbing. I was thirty years old when I met Brian. At that time, he had told me that he was the same age as I was. He had even produced a thirtieth birthday card that he said he had received from his sister, and I had believed him. I later found out from his mam that he was in fact four years younger than me. I was shocked. We argued about him lying, but the relationship carried on regardless. The age gap would have been a problem had I been younger, but it wasn't so much then as I was heading into my thirties.

Brian would stay over a few nights a week until it got to the point that he was a permanent fixture at my flat. Before I knew it, we were talking about buying a house together and we had started to save. We would pool our money and it was lodged into Brian's bank account. I never thought at the time that this would turn out to be a bad idea. I trusted Brian back then and I thought that things would work out for us. Had I known what was in store for me, I never would have taken the risk of parting with my money and letting him take care of things. When I think back, I realise how stupid I really was. I was just excited to be setting up home with Brian and my daughter. The thought of buying a house together was a big step and a commitment, which, at the time, I really wanted to make. It had just been Robyn and me for so long and being a single parent was difficult. At the time I was pleased that we would become a family and I would have support with bringing up Robyn. You think that you know someone, but really you don't.

Brian was really excited about looking for a house. We went to see a bank official about getting a mortgage. As Brian was self-employed as a milkman with Premier Dairies, we also went to see an accountant so that we could give the bank details of Brian's income. We hoped that with the accountant's report and my P60, the bank would consider our application. We were eventually approved for the loan and we began searching for a place.

We viewed a couple of houses before we went to see the cottage. Mitchelstown Cottage stood on a third of an acre on the outskirts of Finglas. It was close to the Meath border. Brian was interested from what he could see from the newspaper clipping that his mam had from one of the local Northside papers.

It was a dark and cold November evening when we went to view the cottage in Kilshane. We travelled along a dark winding road that was lined with trees and badly lit. It was eerie, but in some ways it was quite beautiful. We arrived at the cottage and pulled into a small pebble-stone drive, which you could hear crunch as the wheels of the van rolled over it. Very large conifer trees surrounded the house. From what I could see in the dark, the garden looked well maintained and beautiful. I felt though that the house was very isolated, and I wasn't sure that I would be very comfortable with that. I was used to and enjoyed having people around me. I knew that if we bought this cottage that I would not have people close by.

I was very disappointed when we went inside. It was dirty and old and it stank. I said nothing. I continued on through the house in the hope that it would get better, but it didn't. The rooms were very small. The bathroom was decorated in pink. The wooden windows had rotted away through neglect. The living area stank of urine, and we later discovered that it was used by the previous owner to house dogs. It was awful. I knew it would be a lot to take on. I glanced at Brian occasionally in disgust, but he remained attentive to what the estate agent was saying. Brian was really keen, but I wanted to see other houses before we made an offer.

Brian could see potential in the property. I on the other hand thought that it would be another huge financial drain on us. We would have to find more money to repair and upgrade the cottage. I was worried that we would over-stretch ourselves and that the house would eat up any money we had. Brian had also said that his mam thought that the property would be a very good investment for the future.

After a few days and a few disagreements, we made an offer that was accepted. We moved into the house within a month, bringing all my furniture and belongings with us. Brian's father, William, or Billy, as we called him, who was a carpenter, promised to help us renovate the place. It was a promise that he kept.

We were happy there for a time – until I started to see

a different side of Brian. He had previously had a violent argument with a neighbour of mine over money, before we moved into the cottage. That should have been enough to set alarm bells ringing. The guy was working for Brian delivering milk on Brian's round. Brian had extended the milk round to the block of flats that I lived in. It would bring in more money that we needed for our deposit on the house, and we were under pressure now to reach our target. However, this only went on for a few weeks. It was obvious that the row erupted because of money. It seems that Brian had pulled a fast one on this guy, and had ripped him off in some way by either not paying him a wage or by not sticking to the agreed split of profits at the end of their contract. At the time I believed Brian. He had not given me any reason to doubt him. I also knew that the other guy had a bit of a reputation. How wrong was I? The truth came to light at a later stage. The row was so ferocious that the gardaí were involved. The guy had put my kitchen window through and damaged my front door when he battered it with a baseball bat trying to get to Brian. I was terrified. Brian had punched the guy in the face, which led to him coming to my flat, furious and hell bent on equalling the score. He was like a wild animal trying to get in at Brian.

That week, mid-November 1996, the bank released the mortgage. The owner agreed to let us move into the house earlier than planned. I was delighted, as I was now fearful of even going to the corner shop, because of the fight. Gossip about the row between Brian and this guy had filtered through the block of flats that I lived in, and the feedback that I was receiving was not good. These were not people that you messed with, but who could blame that guy for being angry? I had never had any trouble with the other residents there before. Now I was receiving unwanted and very negative attention. I recall some of the women that lived in the flat complex shouting out the windows at me as I returned from work. They verbally threatened me and told me what they were going to do to me when they got their hands on me. One of the women was this guy's partner, and the other one was her best friend. In all the time that I had lived there with Robyn I had never had a run-in with anyone. I had always kept my head down and minded my own business. Brian had brought this negative attention on me. When we moved to the cottage I was relieved to get away from the stressful situation in the flats. Little did I know that the stress was going to get worse, much worse.

Brian's parents and siblings came and helped us pack

all of our belongings. Brian's friend Peter Kiernan also helped. Peter had a van that we used to transport the furniture to the cottage. When everything was packed away, I felt a sadness closing the door of the flat. I had enjoyed the times that Robyn and I had had there. I hoped that I was not making a mistake. If I was, it was too late to turn back.

During the first few weeks after moving into the house we were happy. So was Robyn. Our relationship in the beginning seemed relatively normal. We seemed to be doing all of the things that any other couple does. We shared some of the chores and we decorated the house together. We also shared the costs of groceries and household bills. Money was tight, but we got by. I thought that we had things under control. Even if it meant that we had sausage, beans and chips for dinner, we didn't complain. Robyn was really taking a shine to Brian, and they seemed to be getting closer. He was good to her. It made me feel better knowing that we could all get along, and that she was happy.

The first winter was hard. The house was cold, we were still decorating and it was tiring. But it was lovely to be out in the countryside and to do things that we hadn't been able to do in the flats. Robyn and I enjoyed our walks in the surrounding fields, and we'd go out blackberry picking. We would also feed carrots to the family of donkeys that we had discovered living at the bottom of Bay Lane. I have happy memories of those times with Robyn.

Brian's father, Billy, came nearly every morning to build the kitchen units and wardrobes, and we would sit chatting for hours, drinking tea. He was a jovial type of man and was down to earth. Brian's mam and his two sisters would also help out with the house by filling the window boxes with fresh flowers and tending some of the plants. I got on well with them in the beginning and appreciated the effort they made helping to turn the cottage into a home for us.

The house was really taking shape. That year passed very quickly – it seemed like no time before we were celebrating our one-year anniversary there. My mam babysat and we went for a drink in Dolly Heffernan's. Although our budget was tight, we could allow ourselves one night out. Brian was still working as a milkman in Premier Dairies and I was still working in the Esso garage. I had returned to work there sometime in 1994 and was working part-time while Robyn was at school. I loved my job and I loved my life – though that was going to change. Brian would make sure of that.

Brian continually had a string of different people turning up at the house. I had never met them before and I was wary of them. All of a sudden there seemed to be an obvious distraction that was pulling Brian's attention away from me. Brian was very taken with his new-found friends and their get-rich-quick schemes. I knew that we had to keep the mortgage under control, but I felt Brian was trying too hard to make more money. He resorted to collecting pallets from nearby industrial estates. He had them piled high in the front garden. They looked terrible at the front of the house. He would receive IR£3-5 per pallet at the end of each week. One of the men that Brian had brought to the house had introduced him to this way of making money.

Brian became obsessed with money and didn't speak of much else. I was beginning to grow a little concerned about him. He was driving himself to the point of exhaustion. He was never happy with what he had. I often wondered where he got his strength from. He was always on the go. There was always something that he had to do. He was so active and busy that he seemed to be constantly hyper.

Brian and his colleague, John [not his real name], continued their pallet collection for some months. John was always at the house; he seemed a nice kind of guy, quite pleasant.

Christmas had passed. We had spent it with Brian's parents and had also visited my family. Life just seemed normal to me then and I was happy. It was early into the New Year, and I was not feeling well. I was tired and I had been vomiting. I went to see the doctor, and she told me that there was a possibility that I was pregnant. I was shocked, especially as I had been taking the pill. We had not planned a pregnancy. When I left the surgery, I was still in shock and decided to buy a pregnancy test. The test came up positive. I did not tell Brian that day, as I didn't know how he would react. Money was tight and a baby would make it tighter. I was still trying to get my head around the idea of having a baby.

I decided to break the news to Brian, and worried a little about what his reaction might be. Although he had expressed his desire for a child on a couple of occasions, I was still a little apprehensive about telling him. Even though we had discussed having children, everything about this relationship was moving too fast: living together, buying the house and now a baby.

It was my day off work and I plodded around cleaning the house. Billy had turned up at the house that morning to do some work. Billy, who was in his mid-fifties, always seemed to like keeping himself busy. I had not been expecting him. I made some coffee and we sat chatting for a while in the kitchen. Billy was a witty man and I enjoyed his company most days. I was glad to see a familiar face stop by, even to say hello, especially as I was quite isolated and away from all my friends and my own family. I had been used to people calling over to see me when I lived in the flats. Billy went outside and removed some tools from the boot of the car. He had decided to get started on building and fitting our new bedroom wardrobes. I was delighted as all our clothes were still in bags or strewn around the bedroom, the dirty mixed with the clean, most of them Brian's. I hated untidiness; sometimes it would drive me to the point of nearly picking them all up and binning them. I couldn't wait to have wardrobes to hang everything up in and to get the bedroom organised and tidy.

It was nearly noon and Brian was due home from work. Billy had been in the cottage since around ten o'clock, sawing and hammering away. I decided to cook some breakfast, and hoped to have it ready before Brian got home. I took some sausages, bacon and eggs from the fridge and went to the cooker to get started. Just then I could hear the crunching of the pebble-stones as Brian's pick-up came onto the driveway. Brian slid open the patio door and walked into the kitchen.

'Jesus, what's this? You're cooking breakfast? What are you looking for?' he said jokingly, as he marched past me and headed into the bedroom to see what Billy was up to. He must have been freezing, as I could feel the cold from him as he passed by me. I continued making breakfast and eavesdropped on their conversation until they joined me in the kitchen. We discussed which way we were going to lay out the bedroom. It was a tight squeeze putting wardrobes in there, as the room only measured eight feet by ten. As we talked, I lifted the cooked sausages and bacon and put them onto three plates. I cracked some eggs into the pan. I don't like eggs very much, and I was beginning to feel slightly quesy at the sight and smell of them as they cooked in the pan, I buttered some bread and made a fresh pot of tea and we all sat down to breakfast. I munched through a bacon sandwich as the others tucked into theirs. Brian had an enormous appetite and was a fast eater. We had no sooner sat down to the meal than I noticed that Brian's plate was nearly cleared. He was wiping his plate with some bread and clearing up the runny yoke that remained on the plate. My stomach heaved as I watched him and I ran to the bathroom to vomit.

'Uh, thanks Rita,' said Brian, as he came into the bathroom, following me in to see if I was OK. I was crouched over the basin. I thought that the vomiting would never stop. Brian stood above me and put his hand on my back, as if to give me reassurance that I would be all right.

'For what'? I asked, knowing too well what he meant.

'For letting me finish breakfast before you decided to do that.' he laughed.

'Very funny,' I said, as I laughed along with him.

'She hasn't given us food poisoning has she, Brian?' Billy shouted, from the kitchen. I knew he was only joking, but I was too ill to respond.

I stood up and went back to take my seat at the table. Brian fetched me a glass of water. Billy looked at me with concern.

'How you feeling now? You must have eaten something that upset you Rita?' Brian added.

Placing my head between my knees and taking deep breaths, I thought to myself, *if only they knew*. I knew what was making me sick.

'She's had the same as we've had, and we're both fine. Must be morning sickness!' Billy said, laughing – not realising he was right.

'Fuck off, you!' Brian laughed at his dad's joke, but then quickly turned his attention back to me. I just gazed back at him and bit my lip.

'Are you? Rita, are you pregnant?' he asked, as if he

really wanted the answer to be yes.

'I didn't want to tell you this way, Brian, but, yes, I am. I only found out yesterday. I was trying to pick the right moment to tell you, but you were so tired last night that I just let you go to bed,' I explained, and watched Brian's face beam with delight at hearing the news.

Brian and I were really excited about having a baby. That week we informed the rest of our families and everyone was delighted with the news and wished us well. I think that Ann, Brian's mam, was over the moon, as it would be her first grandchild (Brian was her firstborn).

❧ ❧

On Thursdays and Fridays I would help Brian out with the milk bill collections. Sometimes Robyn would come along for the ride. We had fun driving in the open-back red pick-up, but it stank of sour milk. The smell could be so bad sometimes that you would still smell it on your clothes the next day – if you were brave enough to put them back on. I could even smell them in the wash basket before I put them in the washing machine. There would be all three of us in the front and about six young lads in the back, messing and joking and screaming obscenities at Brian to wind him up. It was all innocent fun. We would be so tired when we got home, and some of the young lads would be whinging that their feet hurt or were cut, or one poor little fella would be sulking after taking some flack and teasing from his work-mates. But they would all still turn out the following week for the same torture. I suppose it is part of the norm for working-class kids in Dublin.

I remember as a child growing up, working in the bulb fields in St Margarets's all day long for pocket money, and then spending it all in the farmer's shop before I went home. Got it in one hand, gave it back with the other. During the summer holidays, the farmer would wait each morning at the bottom of McKelvey Avenue in his tractor and trailer, and wait for the kids to pile in. It was a novelty to us back then, even if it meant that we would spend most of the day on our hands and knees sifting through the clay and filling the buckets with bulbs. We thought it was fun. The money that we received was pitiful. It probably cost my mam more to replace the clothes that we destroyed, as they would get covered in mud. Those years were the best years of my life, so I guess some of these kids will look back someday and probably have similar memories of the fun they had working on the milk round.

On a few occasions I went to Premier Dairies on the Finglas Road with Brian so that he could drop back any unwanted milk or pay a milk bill at the end of the week. I don't think that he was popular in the dairy yard. I remember on a couple of occasions a few of the helpers on different milk agents' rounds referred to Brian as 'Johnny Handsome'. When I asked Brian what they meant he was reluctant to answer. He didn't look too happy about their comments. After giving it a couple of minutes thought, it was obvious to me that they were slagging him. Brian would not have been considered good looking. He suffered with very bad acne as a teenager, which left his face very badly scared.

The first few months in the cottage had passed quickly. Brian and John were still collecting pallets and our front drive was full of them. I hated the look of them piled outside the house. As it was not illegal to collect them, I thought it was fine, until one evening Brian and John went out late in the evening and came back to the house hours later with both pick-ups piled high with pallets. They were laughing and joking. It later came to light that they had stolen them from a pallets yard on the south side of Dublin. When they had offloaded all the pallets from both of the vans and Brian had invited John in for tea in the kitchen, both of them still laughing, I discovered exactly what they had been up to as they talked openly about stealing the pallets. I couldn't believe they had robbed them. I was furious, but my objections went unheard. Brian and John seemed really pleased with themselves. I left them to it – laughing and joking in the kitchen.

They were spending a lot of time together and I thought that Brian was becoming a bit distant and disrespectful with me. I remember one night we were both in bed and I was just about to fall asleep when I was startled by the roar of an engine and bright lights shining in through the bedroom window. I jumped up out of the bed, but Brian told me to relax as it was only John.

'What the hell is he doing here at this time of night?' I snapped.

'Go back asleep. He'll be gone in a few minutes,' Brian barked back at me.

I lay back down on the bed, but I got up after a few minutes because I wanted to see what was going on. As I entered the kitchen I could see John unwrap what looked like a sod of turf. It was in fact a bar of hash. He did not even acknowledge me. They continued talking as if I wasn't there. John opened the microwave, placed the bar of hash inside it and then turned it on. I could not believe my eyes. He then took it out and cut it in half with a large breadknife and handed half to Brian. He placed the other half in his coat pocket, put back on his motorbike helmet, and, as quick as he had arrived, he was gone. What were they thinking? What had Brian got himself involved in?

'What are you doing Brian? That's hash?' I asked.

'It's just a bit of blow that John got me for Paddy [not his real name],' Brian explained.

Paddy was one of Brian's friends. Straight away I knew that he was lying. Paddy would never involve himself in anything like that. Paddy's and Brian's lifestyles were worlds apart. Not only was it a lie, it was a bad lie. We argued for a while and then went back to bed. I still couldn't believe that Brian was doing this and that he was so relaxed about it. I was so angry. I didn't get much sleep that night.

The following morning I got up and went to the bathroom. As I looked in the mirror I could see that my baby was growing. My tummy was beginning to squeeze out through my pyjama buttons. I was looking forward to meeting this little person. Brian had gone to work during the night to deliver the milk. I was still fuming about John's visit the night before. I got dressed and brought Robyn to school. Later that evening, I discussed the hash with Brian. He told me that it was a one off. I really hoped so. Unfortunately, it wasn't.

Over the coming weeks, this recurred a couple of times. As a result, Brian and I were arguing a lot. Things were getting bad and I was beginning to worry a lot. I didn't want drugs in my home, especially with Robyn in the house and a baby on the way. I was also worried about the change in Brian. He was beginning to show a side of himself that I had never seen before. Some days I tried to humour him, especially when I thought that he was getting agitated with something.

I never really knew much about Brian's past; he never gave much away about it. I remember his mother telling me of an incident that occurred when Brian was a young teen. He had been drinking with friends and had got himself into a state of oblivion. She told me that he stole an ambulance from a northside hospital. He had driven it out of the hospital grounds and crashed it. Luckily, nobody was injured but himself. The gardaí were called. I don't know if he was arrested or fined, or if, because of his age, he just received a caution. It was never spoken about after that. I never brought it up with Brian. She also told me about an incident that occurred on the school grounds when Brian was a student. His mam had been called to the school because Brian was causing problems. He had managed to force another pupil's head through the metal railings that surrounded the school grounds. The fire brigade had to be called to free the boy. I remember Brian laughing as his mam told me the story. At the time I put it down to adolescent stupidity. I guess that there were many more stories that I was never told. Brian's past seemed to be very deeply buried and forgotten.

Even though there was some tension between us, we were looking forward to having a new family member. Robyn was looking forward to having a brother or sister at last. She had always wanted one and always wanted to be a big sister. I knew she'd make a wonderful big sister. I was glad she was so pleased about my pregnancy. Though I was excited about the baby, I was growing increasingly worried that Brian was going to land himself in deeper trouble, possibly with the gardaí.

The next couple of months passed and everything was going well with the pregnancy. I was taking care of myself: eating the right foods, keeping my ante-natal appointments and resting when I could. I continued to work though, and my colleagues took it easy with me. They were very supportive. They covered some of my chores when my tummy started to expand outwards so that I could not bend and would eventually not be able to see my feet. They had a great time jeering me over that. I went on maternity leave in September and had every intention to return to work when my leave was over.

I continued to work alongside Brian collecting the milk money every Thursday and Friday. Joseph O'Callaghan (Joey) was one of the young lads that collected the money with us. He was a pleasant young lad, and I really took a liking to him. We laughed a lot together. Joey and I covered the Porterstown and Clonsilla areas. We would make our way on foot, knocking door to door. We always had a laugh when we worked together. But it was getting harder for me to walk as my due date approached. I had to stop going on the milk collections. I was no longer able for the long walks as I found them exhausting. I'll always remember doing those rounds with Joey. He was good company.

Brian continued with his milk round and young Joey helped out. Joey delivered the milk in the mornings before school and over the weekends he helped Brian to collect the milk money. Brian had brought Joey to our house on a couple of ocassions and sometimes he would share breakfast with us before heading home to Blakestown. Brian had also started to bring young Joey out with him in his search of pallets. John was still showing up at the house, but now it was just the odd time. John and Brian discussed the pallets but I never heard hashish being brought into the conversation from that point onwards. I was glad. I hoped that was the last of it.

Sometime in October, late one evening, a young man named Paul [not his real name] came to visit Brian. He worked with Brian at the dairy yard. Immediately, I knew something was wrong. I could tell he had some kind of addiction. His eyes were deep-set, his face was drawn and his speech slurred. I did not know much about drugs. I had only ever taken Anadin and aspirin, and I was sure that this guy was on neither. Then came the all too familiar sound: Brian's explanation. He told me Paul had fallen out with his dad and that he was putting him up for the night. I did not want a complete stranger staying in my home, and was not happy that Brian seemed fine about it. I didn't like the way that he was putting a junkie's well-being before Robyn's and mine. He was bringing a strange man into what was supposed to be the safe environment of my home, and my little girl was sleeping less than twenty feet away from him. I was heavily pregnant and felt very vulnerable. Brian would be heading out on his milk round at about 3.00 a.m. He said that he would bring Paul with him. I went to bed feeling disgusted. I lay awake until I heard the two leave during the night: keeping one ear on them and the other on Robyn.

Brian didn't come home from work the next day or that night. I was getting worried as he was not answering his phone. Luckily for me, I had recently bought myself a new mobile phone, just in case of an emergency. I was left isolated with no means of communication with anyone.

I had no neighbours to run to and no transport. I slept in the nursery that night, upright on a wicker chair with my legs propped between the bars of the cot. The nursery faced onto the forecourt and the pebble-stone drive. I sat in the dark, and watched and waited until I eventually fell asleep. I awoke the next morning to the noise of keys tapping loudly on the window. It was Brian's dad, Billy. It was pouring rain outside, so I made my way quickly to the back door to let him in. I was really stiff from sleeping in the chair. I knew he was wondering why I had slept there, and as there was no sign of Brian's pick-up, he put two and two together. He also tried to reach Brian on his phone and got no reply. I made some tea, and we sat and chatted and waited for Brian to return.

Billy stayed with us until late into the day. I did not send Robyn to school that day. I didn't want to leave the house for fear that something bad had happened to Brian. Billy didn't seem that worried. He was confident that Brian would return in one piece. It was five o'clock in the afternoon when Billy decided to head home. He told me to ring him if there was any problem. Robyn sat at the kitchen table slowly putting together a Barbie jigsaw. I laughed to myself, as she lost her temper through her confusion, and tried to force the pieces into place with her tiny fist. I had the dinner on the cooker; everything was just about ready – potatoes, broccoli, peas and lamb chops. There was still no sign of Brian. I tried to reach him on the phone, to let him know that dinner was ready, but I got no reply. It was six o'clock when we sat down to dinner. I saved some for Brian, and put it aside so that he could have it later.

I could not understand Brian's behaviour at all. He had become distant and unconcerned. Things were going all right for us both, or so I thought, but I could see changes in our relationship. Sometimes I blamed the pregnancy, thinking that maybe Brian was growing a bit anxious about the birth and his new responsibility. Other times I blamed my hormones. I also knew that things were not always running smoothly with the dairy; some weeks the amount of milk that customers needed would be up, and some weeks down. Although there was always cash flow through the week, there was always an outstanding bill at the end of it too. Like everyone else, we had good weeks and we had bad.

The hours passed and still there was no sign of Brian. Robyn had gone to bed. I was still sitting watching television when I heard the wheels of Brian's van come into the drive. I tried to lift myself out of the chair to head to the back door to greet him, but before I could get up, he raced into the living room with his head in his hands – he was crying.

I was pleading with him for an explanation. Still crying, he told me that I would not believe what he had just witnessed. He told me that he had been with Paul and that Paul had nearly overdosed on heroin. For a moment I thought that he was going to tell me about some terrible accident, but to me this was shocking. We were shouting at each other now. I asked him why he was with Paul. Was he taking drugs? He said he wasn't. I asked him what was his interest in Paul. I wanted to know, and I was afraid that my intuition was correct. I thought, *first the hash and now this*. When I accused him of dealing, he went ballistic and got very defensive.

We were still shouting at each other as he made his way quickly to the back door with me following him. In my frustration I picked up an ornament and threw it in his direction, deliberately missing him. It hit the wall, knocking a large piece of plaster to the ground.

What came next was unforeseen. I could see Brian's expression change as he lunged forward and grabbed me by the hair. Then I felt his hand come down hard on my face. He loosened his grip on my hair and tossed my head to the side. I lost balance and fell across the dining table and chair. Robyn had been woken up by all the shouting and screaming. She was standing at her bedroom door, crying as she witnessed her mammy being attacked. I could hear her cries, but I couldn't go to her, as Brian still had me at his mercy. I pleaded and pleaded with him to let me go. I was in agony and so frightened. I wanted to comfort Robyn, but most of all I wanted this nightmare to end.

He was like a wild animal. He took my hand and twisted it, burning the skin around my wrist. It really hurt. I was in a lot of pain.

'Let go, let go. You'll break my hand!' I screamed. Tears were rolling down my face. I was traumatised by Brian's violence.

'I won't; I know how far to push it before the bone snaps!' he sneered at me. 'You whinging bitch,' he growled, before finally letting go of my hand. I couldn't believe what had just happened. The man who was supposed to love me had attacked me – in front of my daughter. The father of my child had beaten me when I was carrying his unborn child.

He left and went into our bedroom, closing the door behind him. Robyn came and knelt beside me, still sobbing. She gently stroked my hair with her little hand to sooth me. I noticed that bunches of my hair were coming away in her hand and she was looking at me with a frightened look on her little face. How did this happen?

Why did this happen? I was shocked. I was saddened. I was horrified. I was also in a lot of pain and sick with worry about my baby. Had the beating hurt my baby?

Brian left the house that night and arrived back the next morning after he had finished his milk round. But he was late. Billy had arrived at the house before him. We sat in the kitchen chatting. I never mentioned the attack on me the night before, and I told Robyn not to say anything either. We were both still in shock and comforting one another. Billy asked why Robyn was not in school. He then realised that Brian had not arrived home in time. He offered to bring her, and I accepted. I also told him that I had my antenatal appointment later that morning. He offered to take me if Brian had not returned by then. It was then that I heard Brian's van pull into the drive. He came into the kitchen by the patio doors and sheepishly looked at me. He was probably wondering if I had said anything to his dad. After a few seconds he realised that I hadn't, and he let out a sigh. He looked at his watch and told me that it was nearly time for my appointment at the maternity hospital. He said he'd just get himself ready and would then bring me.

Billy took Robyn to school in his car, and Brian and I headed for the maternity hospital.

The journey into town was quiet, with neither of us

saying much. I was anxious to get the doctors to examine me as I was worried about the night before. I prayed that my baby was OK. I was about five-and-a-half months regnant, and I worried that my baby may be affected by my stress.

Thankfully, I got the all clear from the doctors. Everthing seemed fine: my blood pressure and bloods were all normal. I remember feeling relief as I left the hospital, but I also remember feeling upset and let down and also quite vulnerable. The journey home was also silent. Brian dropped me back to the cottage. Before he left he told me that he would collect Robyn from school later that day. I was relieved that my baby was OK, but I was still numb with shock. I couldn't believe what had happened the night before.

At some stage later in the day, Brian arrived home with a huge bunch of flowers. He cried and begged for forgiveness. He also pleaded with Robyn, and treated her to a McDonald's Happy Meal, which she discarded on the kitchen chair. She barely touched it. We had all lost our appetites that day.

Life continued as normal for the rest of the week, with Brian on his best behaviour. He couldn't do enough: fixing up the house and yard, running errands and so on. Nevertheless, deep down I still felt the hurt and my trust in him was gone for good. I knew that I would never look at Brian in the same way. My respect for him was gone. I felt like I was walking on eggshells and that he could explode at any minute. I was now very wary of him. Despite this I didn't think of leaving at that point. I was heavily pregnant and felt that I was in a very vulnerable situation. Where would I run to? I prayed that it was only a one-off attack and that it would never happen again. I had never seen that aggressive side of Brian before and neither had Robyn. I found myself trying to make sense of what had happened and I tried to reassure Robyn that everything would be OK. It was the first time that Brian had attacked me – but it was not going to be the last.

Over the coming months, as my vulnerability became apparent to Brian, his control and abuse became more pronounced. As the weeks passed there was a lot of activity at the house, with Brian's friends, Peter Joyce and Peter Kiernan, coming and going a lot. He worked with both of them in Premier Dairies. I knew that they were up to no good. John 'the pallet man' was still hanging around. I was surprised by Brian's dad; he was also showing an interest in whatever plan Brian was concocting. I knew that it had to be something dodgy. I had a feeling whatever they were up to was not good. I knew it was another of their get-rich-quick schemes. Brian's father's involvement was only endorsing what Brian was doing. At the time, I wished he had encouraged Brian to not get involved. I didn't stand a chance when it came to airing my concerns. They were too blinded by the easily acquired cash now available to them.

It was October and we were still rowing. I couldn't understand what was happening to us. I couldn't understand why he was ruining what we had: a new home, a baby on the way and a lovely girl. I had been happy, but I had been blind and I felt fooled. I felt that he had been pulling the wool over my eyes all this time, luring me into a false sense of security. He had built up my dreams, then knocked them all down. And he enjoyed doing it.

Our house was constantly full of Brian's friends, scheming and plotting new ways to make money. I never knew where Brian was. Robyn's home life was affected. I knew that my little girl was worrying. She would often snuggle up to me on the couch, and ask why Brian was doing the things that he was doing. Robyn would not have known about the hash, but she understood clearly that Brian had stolen the pallets on the forecourt. At such a young age, that would have worried her. Children need to feel protected, not afraid, as she clearly was. This was not how I had planned our life in our new home to turn out.

I never heard another word spoken about Paul and I often wondered what had happened to him. It was apparent to me that Brian had actually been using Paul, as he would have been able to teach Brian how to cut and bag either heroin or cocaine. He would also be able to shine some light on how to close a drug deal, and, how he could evade the gardaí. Brian had known nothing about drugs in the beginning, but Paul clearly did. There was no other reason why Brian would have associated with him.

ഈ ര

I was nearing my due date. I had a hospital appointment on 20 November 1997, and Brian and Robyn came with me. I brought my overnight bag – just in case.

When they did tests, my urine sample had showed protein content. The doctor advised me that he was concerned because protein had been detected at my last two visits and no one had noted it. During pregnancy, too much protein in the urine over a period of time is an indication that something is wrong internally and that the body is not filtering its waste properly. Too much protein in the urine of a pregnant woman can lead to problems with the liver, kidneys and the brain and can also lead to edema and high blood pressure, which is dangerous. The doctor told me that he was going to admit me, and that I would possibly have to have the labour induced.

I stayed in the hospital to have more tests done, and Brian went to the pick-up to bring me my bag that I had packed. It contained my pyjamas and toiletries. By the time he got back to me, the doctor had me in a ward and had instructed the nurses that my waters where to be broken and that I was to be put on a synotinocin, which was a drip to move my labour along. Things were at last beginning. I was so excited to meet my baby, but I was also afraid and hoped that everything would be all right. Brian left the hospital and brought Robyn to my mother's home. He promised that he would come straight back to me. It seemed like forever, as I paced the corridors in excruciating pain.

Then he was back and I was relieved. Brian was holding me up, as I stooped in agony. He encouraged me, praised me and reassured me. The midwife was terrific. She did everything in her power to make me as comfortable as possible. But the pain was becoming unbearable. It got so bad that I lost track of time. Eventually, I was brought into the labour room. I could see a large black mattress on the ground. Everyone in the room helped to get me down onto the floor and make me as comfortable as they could. I was crying in pain and begging for help. I thought that I was going to die.

My cervix had fully dilated, but this child did not want to come out. The doctor and the midwife held my legs apart as I screamed in agony. Both of them encouraged me to push. Brian sat on the mattress with his arms around my back, holding both of my hands and speaking words of encouragement, but still this child would not be born. I begged the doctor for a caesarean section, as I felt that something was wrong, but he refused. He then reached for an object made of shinny metal. I could not make out what it was until the doctor placed it between my legs and began to pull with force at my baby's head.

It was at this moment that Brian turned to me, apologised and left the room. He could watch no more. *Not now!*. I thought I really didn't want him to leave me at that point. The doctor continued to pull at my child's head and I became increasingly alarmed by this. I was overwhelmed with fear for my baby's life. At that point the midwife pushed the doctor away from me shaking her head. Even through my pain I understood that they were arguing about what the next step should be. The midwife was demanding that I have a caesarean section: the caesarean section that I had pleaded for twenty-eight hours earlier.

I do not remember much else after that. The last memory I have was being brought in a lift to a bright room and being surrounded with masked people, all dressed in green. One doctor quickly examined my chest. As he did, he questioned the doctor who had been attending to me and asked if he had noted a murmur on my heart.

'Anyone detected a murmur on her heart?' he asked, panicking.

'No,' came a faint answer from the corner of the room from the doctor who was now standing aside and watching in awe.

'Well she has one now!' he added, sounding alarmed.

The events that followed over the coming days after the birth of my baby boy, Conor, were completely foreign to me. I had had a bad time. I was on life support in a different hospital in the city, and my baby had remained in the special care unit of the maternity hospital. Conor was three days old and he had not met his mammy yet. We both needed a cuddle.

I remember opening my eyes and trying to focus on what was in front of me. I was frightened when I realised where I was. The machines that were keeping me alive were all around me making funny noises. I could see what was like a glass window in front of me and behind that glass was a small room. I could see a person move about and they eventually came out of the room and stood beside me.

'Hello Rita. Don't be frightened. You have not been well and we have been taking care of you. Your family have been here with you all of the time and they will be back again later. I am going to ask the doctor to come and see you, OK? You rest.'

I watched as she left the room. I did not want to be left alone. I did not want to die alone. I couldn't call her because of the tubes running down through my mouth and body. I could feel tears run down my face. I couldn't move any part of my body, not even to lift my little finger. I tried to make out who else was in the room with me. As I peered to each side of me, I knew I was not alone. There were about four other beds in this tiny room. All of these people were just as sick as I was. They were also being kept alive by machines.

The nurse returned to the room, but with a priest, not a doctor. He stood over me praying and anointing me. I remember I wanted to tell him to go away – how dare he assume I was going to die. I wanted to scream, but I couldn't. Then they left. I fought to keep my eyes open, I was afraid to fall into unconsciousness and never wake up again. I wanted so much to see my baby. I didn't know if I had given birth to a girl or a boy, or indeed if the child was also fighting to survive. I fought long and hard to stay awake, but at some point I drifted off again. But just before I nodded off, I spotted a small photograph on top of one of the machines. It was the first glimpse of my new baby, wrapped in a blue blanket. It was a boy. He was OK. I was so relieved. I had wanted to dismiss God earlier, but now I wanted to embrace him for sparing my child's life.

I would never have imagined going through such pain during Conor's birth. I had endured childbirth before with Robyn, of course, and went through some difficulty, which led to a caesarean section. However, on Robyn's birth my recovery was quick, plus I had youth on my side. I was older having Conor; there was an eight-year gap between the two births.

I was taken back to the maternity hospital after the general hospital had stabilised me. They had planned to send me for convalescence in a clinic in North Dublin. However, they discovered that I had contracted MRSA and that ruled that out. The maternity hospital had to put me into a private room. The television was always on and I couldn't move to reach for the remote control. The doctors and nurses checked on me regularly; they tried their best to keep me comfortable.

Over the coming days, I started to recover gradually.

It was not easy. I had eventually been reunited with my son, but I had not been able to look after him as I wanted to. I could not pick him up without help from the nurses; they had to place Conor on my chest so that I could feel close to him. I was still very ill indeed. I was always fearful if the nurses left the room that Conor would roll out of my arms and I would not be able to catch him. I had no strength.

I also learned that the doctors had operated on me. I had undergone a hysterectomy. That upset me a lot because it meant that I would never be able to give birth again. I no longer had that choice. It felt as if my womanhood had been taken away from me. The doctors explained to me the difficulties that had resulted in the hysterectomy being performed. They said it was in order to save my life. I had been bleeding internally for a long period after the caesarean section and had suffocated in my own fluids. In order for them to resuscitate me, they had tried to locate the bleeding and isolate it, but in doing so my uterus was affected. I was lucky to have my life.

Conor spent most of the first and second week in the neonatal intensive care unit (NICU) in the maternity hospital. I was unable to get out of bed to go and visit him, even though he was only on the floor above me. I could not move my body. Conor was doing well; there were no further complications with his health. The doctor had advised me that he could be taken home by a family member. Brian's mam volunteered, but I declined her offer as I did not want anybody else bonding with him before I could.

One morning I woke up feeling a lot of pain in my abdomen. Although I was on a lot of painkillers, none of them seemed to be numbing this pain. I was so sick that I was unable to reach for the bell that was hanging on the bedpost above my head. I tried to call out, but the door to my room was closed and no one could hear me. Then, to my horror, as I lay limp in the bed, the crisp white cotton sheet turned into blotting paper. I watched in terror as my blood was soaked up by the sheets. I was so scared, but I couldn't even move my hands to lift the sheets to see where it was coming from. I remember I started to scream and call for help. The TV was still on and the volume was quite high.

I screamed and screamed through desperation and with what little strength I had, I managed to get a grip of a hairbrush that a nurse had left on the bed that morning after washing me. Using all my strength I managed to fling it at the door. I continued screaming until a number of people burst through the door. Among them was my doctor. He had been doing his rounds that morning and he was accompanied by about three or four nurses. I thanked God that someone had heard me. The doctor tried to calm me and lifted the sheets to have a better look. I was afraid to look at first. When I did I was even more horrified, as I could see my intestines were trying to burst out through the scar tissue. I could sense the doctor's panic. They immediately put me on an intravenous drip and they prepared the area for further surgery, cleaning and dressing it. The doctor then left the room and told me that he would be back shortly.

When the doctor returned, he told me that I was going to be sent to St Vincent's Hospital, in Donnybrook. He explained that the wound had dehiscenced and would have to be repaired. He said that it would be a dangerous operation because the wound might not repair and also because I would have to go under another general anaesthetic. This meant that I would have had three general anaesthetics very close together. The thought of the operation and the risks involved terrified me.

An ambulance came quickly and brought me to St Vincent's. They took me into the intensive care department where the staff rallied around me quickly. It was then that I saw my mam and my sister Mary arrive. The doctors explained to them what was about to happen.

I knew that they were both apprehensive. I knew what I was facing now. I had made it through the last time, but this time I might not be as lucky. I said my goodbyes to them and prayed to God to save my soul. I could see mam and Mary fade into the distance as the porter wheeled me into the operating theatre. I remember crying.

I have never really believed in near-death experiences. I have always remained a little sceptical on that subject. I've had my doubts when I've heard stories about people who find themselves at death's door, in some sort of tunnel of light in the presence of angels or spirits. I can only explain what happened next as a beautiful dream. I found myself surrounded by a beautiful calming light. There was no tunnel. I remember that I saw my late father in the distance. I was delighted to see him and started to run towards him to hug him, but as I was running I realised that I was not getting any closer to him. I remember feeling overwhelmed with joy, I was so happy. He stood there without moving; he had his hands in his pockets and he was smiling at me. He didn't beckon me to come any closer to him or greet me with outstretched arms; he just smiled at me. Then a small dark-haired woman linked my left arm and led me away from him. I was protesting and trying to get away from her. I wanted to go to my father but she wouldn't let me. She told me that we needed to go in a different direction and insisted that we move away. I was waving at my dad and trying to make him understand that this woman was not letting me get any nearer. He remained smiling at me while he faded into the distance. Then I was back in the darkness. I've never dreamt of him since.

Thankfully, the operation was a success. My recovery was a bit slow though. I could not eat, and as much as the dietician offered me different foods, I still didn't feel like eating. After undergoing three general anaesthetics, my tongue was like sandpaper and food felt like razor blades. The doctors were worried. I wasn't eating and they needed me to so that I could build up my strength. They decided to put me on a feeder drip. This meant that I would have a drip that ran up my nose and into my stomach. It sounds disgusting but it saved my life.

My family and Brian's family visited both Conor and me everyday. They were very supportive and encouraging. Brian visited too. He was delighted with his new son. On a few occasions he failed to show up, but he would ring me and make his excuses. I suspected that he was up to no good, but all I really cared about was my baby son and my body recovering. All I wanted was to get home for Christmas to celebrate it as a family: Brian and me and our two children, Robyn and Conor. I missed Robyn and I knew that she was missing me too. I knew that she was safe and well, as she was staying with my mam. My family looked after her when Mam wanted to visit the hospital to see me.

❧ ☙

It was a week before Christmas when the doctors gave me the all clear to go home. I was feeling stronger and couldn't wait to get out of that institution that had been my home for five weeks. Brian seemed to be in a hurry to get us out of there too, and I welcomed his enthusiasm. So I quickly packed all my belongings and we left with our beautiful new arrival.

When I got home to the cottage, Brian opened the back door to the house and let us in ahead of him. I was surprised when I saw that the kitchen had been redecorated with new doors and wallpaper. It looked so cheerful. The wallpaper was burnt orange. It was bright and warm. I could smell the paint from the freshly painted white doors. I was delighted. Brian could tell from my face that I was pleased.

I settled back in after my long absence and I soon had my routine in order. The kids and I were back together, and although I was still in a great deal of pain, I soldiered on. I was looking forward to Christmas Eve. It was my favourite day of the year. Brian had taken me shopping for Christmas presents. But he was distant and had been absent and unsupportive in the week leading up to Christmas. I wondered what was wrong. I felt that there was something going on, as Brian had been spending a lot of time with his friends. He told me that he would not be at home on St Stephen's Day as he had made plans to go to the races at Leopardstown that day with his friend Peter. I told him that I wasn't happy about his plans, but he didn't seem bothered.

It was Christmas, we had a new baby and I was also celebrating having my life and my health back, so I wanted this Christmas to be special. It was obviously special to me, but to Brian it seemed like he was once again caught up in himself and would continue to just suit himself. Once he was happy, nothing else mattered. I felt very sad over Christmas and I waited for St Stephen's day to come. I wanted to see if he would change his mind and spend it at home with his family. I said nothing that morning. I watched him as he groomed himself and left the house. I sobbed when he left. I couldn't believe it. I was barely able to look after myself, let alone our new baby, and he didn't seem to give a damn.

After Brian had left I decided to pull myself together. I washed and put my make-up on and fixed my hair, just in case I had any visitors later in the day. When I was finished, I inspected myself in the mirror. I was pleased: I looked good, despite feeling weak. My hair was cut short to about shoulder length and coloured a warm blonde. I had bought a Chinese-style maroon dress for Christmas that was figure-hugging from the neck to the floor. It was beautiful, and I thought that I looked beautiful in it. I did.

I felt quite lonely and the day passed slowly. I spent it playing with Robyn, while the baby slept. However, I was depressed and in pain, a lot of pain. Brian didn't call once that day to see if we were OK. He didn't care. Robyn went to bed shortly after seven. I decided to have a beer. Only one turned to two, two to three and three to four, and soon I was intoxicated. I should not have been drinking. I was still on medication. A lot of medication: exactly forty-two tablets a day. I don't know what I was thinking of. I guess I was lonely and depressed and thought drinking would help me feel better.

When Brian eventually came home I was still feeling upset over his lack of attention, especially as I had made an effort to look good. He told me about the great day that he had. I was slightly jealous of his newfound freedom, so much so that I told him how I felt, which did not go down well. We got in to a heated argument, shouting obscenities at one another. I had forgotten about Brian's reaction the last time we were in this situation. He didn't like being confronted. His immediate reaction would be to lash out. And that's exactly what he did. He punched me and knocked me unconscious. When I came to, he had placed me on the kitchen table and was trying to bring me around.

Robyn still remembers that night. For the second time she had witnessed Brian's rage. She was terrified. She later told me that Brian was pacing around the house with his head in his hands, frightened and crying. She remembers sitting holding me in her arms. She said Brian was really scared and was frightened that he had killed me. I can't imagine how awful it must have been for Robyn to see me like that. She was only eight – too young to witness something so horrific. Brian called his parents on the phone and they arrived at the cottage shortly afterwards. I don't know what he told them, as I had been unconscious for some time. However, I believe that they tried to reassure Robyn that her mammy would be OK.

'Come on, Rita. Don't do this to me!' Brian shouted as I lay limp on the table. Robyn says she demanded that they call an ambulance. When it arrived at the cottage, Brian's mam promised to stay overnight until we had returned from the hospital. Brian continued to try to revive me. He was pleading with me that I could not die on him. I was taken to James Connolly Hospital in Blanchardstown. I was brought to A&E and the doctors and nurses were quick to see to me.

I remember the worry on Brian's face as the doctors examined me. I also remember the disgusted look a young nurse gave Brian, which made him immediately feel awkward. I knew from the nurse's facial expression that she was not taken in by Brian's explanation. When I gave her my most recent medical history she seemed horrified. She stared at Brian and gave him a look, which made him back away from my bedside. The doctor questioned me about how I had hurt my head. I told him that I had banged it against the door after drinking too much. He said that he thought it was a difficult area to harm from a fall as it was aound the temple. He also seemed concerned for my welfare.

I must have been in the hospital until the early hours of the morning before the doctors discharged me and I went home. I never mentioned the attack that night to any other living soul. In a way I think that I pretended that it had never happened. I just wanted to recover from it and forget about it. Even though the Kennys knew about the incident it was never discussed further or ever mentioned again.

The following weeks were hard for me and I was struggling. I was in so much pain and Brian's beating had added to it. The district nurse was visiting me daily to change my dressings and check on Conor. My GP also called to the house. I never mentioned the violence to her, as I was afraid to and I didn't think that she would be able to help me in any way, other than offering me counselling. Everyone else seemed concerned for me, everyone except Brian. He had changed so much. I didn't know him anymore.

༄ ༄

The house was like Paddington Station again with the constant flow of people coming and going. Some of them were strangers, others were familiar faces – faces that I didn't particulary want to see. Brian was stealing from wherever he could and was missing from home quite a lot. Then on 5 February 1998 I received a phone call to say that Brian had been arrested for drug trafficking and was being held in Whitehall garda station. Brian had dealt drugs to an undercover garda, somewhere in

Drumcondra. He was followed and intercepted with the rest of the gang in a house in Gracepark, in Whitehall. He was being held with three other men who were also involved. They had been arrested and charged with possessing IR£5,000 (€6,350) worth of heroin. One of his co-accused was his father, Billy. The other two were Peter Kiernan and Peter Joyce. I didn't know what to do.

The four were charged and they all appeared in court. I think the rest of the Kenny family were in shock at the revelation. I remember Brian's sister was very worried about what people would think. Brian's mam was too afraid to attend, so I volunteered. It was July 1999 by the time the case came to the Dublin Circuit Criminal Court. I had never been inside a courtroom before and I was nervous. I watched as the gardaí gave their evidence and I listened to the prosecutor. A five-year suspended sentence was handed down to each of the four. I thought that the sentence was very lenient. However, the judge, Elizabeth Dunne, explained to the court that she thought that they were an unusual group of people to come before the courts on drugs charges, as none of them had any previous convictions.

I thought that Brian would be relieved and grateful for escaping a spell in prison and that he would mend his ways. He did for a time, but within weeks he was back to his old ways. Once again he was stealing from industrial estates, and he also started stealing machinery from nearby businesses. Peter Kiernan had moved on with his life and seemed to be steering clear of trouble. But Brian and Peter Joyce were lifting anything that wasn't nailed down.

I remember on one occasion they arrived at the house with a mini-digger. Not long after, two gardaí arrived at the house. Brian stood in the garden speaking to them. I could hear them occasionally laugh, which I thought odd. The gardaí left without the digger. These two gardaí would become a familiar sight at the cottage in Kilshane. I think that Brian thought that he had received a passport to organised crime and could do as he liked. He seemed to be in regular contact with them, and things were about to escalate. He was out of control.

Brian, Peter Kiernan and Peter Joyce were all working for Premier Dairies when they were arrested on drugs charges. All three had to resign their positions, which meant that Brian was now unemployed. I remember the newspaper reports at the time depicting them as milk-distributing drug dealers who delivered more than just a pint of milk on their rounds. I also remember the shame and embarrassment that I felt. Now that Brian's income from the milk round was gone, he would have to find a new way to make money. I knew that he had no intention of getting a regular job.

ꕤ ꕤ

I was still sick and attending doctors. I had been for further tests as I had been in excruciating pain. The pain would come and go, and would immobilise me when it struck. Conor was about four months old now and he was healthy, thank God. I recall being very ill on one occasion. Anybody that has experienced gallbladder pain will know what I am talking about. It is unbearable. I was curled up in a ball on the living room floor, pleading for Brian to help me. But he just stepped over me and without saying a word left the house by the back door. I was left to battle my pain alone.

My maternity leave had ended, but because of my poor health, I was put on disability benefit as I was unfit to work. I had planned on going back to my job, but my bad health was stopping me. For that reason I resigned. I also did not want to part with my new baby son. I was so glad to at least have my life and my healthy new son that everything else seemed unimportant to me at that time.

Chapter Three

The End of the Affair

One afternoon I was at home when there was a knock at the front door. When I looked out through the front window I could see a man I did not recognise. I went to greet him by the back door and met him half way on the drive. I said hello, and he then explained that he was looking for 'Brian the milkman'. He explained that he was a customer of Brian's and he told me that he owed Brian some money. I offered to give him Brian's phone number. He took it and then left.

He was gone juat a couple of minutes, when I saw him return to the drive, so I went back out to him. He explained that he was not there because of money and that he thought that I had a right to know that my husband had been screwing around with his wife. I was gob-smacked. He told me that he had spoken to his wife and that she had told him everything. In the time that the man had left and returned to my door, he had called Brian and told him that he was going to tell me about them as I had a right to know. Brian had begged him not too. The man took my phone number and told me that he would have his wife call me later to confirm his story.

When she called, she told me that she hadn't known that I existed. She and her husband had been apart for a while and had only recently got back together. Brian was causing problems for them. He had called into their house on a few occasions, and she had told him that she was now back together with her husband. From what I could make out from our conversation, the affair had started early during my pregnancy. She had only found out about me when Brian spoke candidly about me and told her that I was on a life support machine. She was horrified and ended the affair.

When Brian arrived I could tell by his face that he wasn't sure if I had been told anything or if indeed the guy had been at the house at all. I could hear another car pull into the drive. It was Ann, Brian's mam. Her timing could not have been better. She came in through the back door, and before either of them spoke, I told Ann that I needed a lift somewhere and that Brian would be coming with us. When she asked me where we were going, I told her that Brian would know the address. He looked at me in disbelief and disgust. I was going to make his mam drive to that woman's house with Brian. Brian's mam was getting the picture.

When we arrived at the house the couple were not there, but the grandmother was. Brian stayed in the back of the car. I asked the old lady if she knew who the guy in the car was and she acknowledged that it was Brian. And so did the many children that were playing in the garden. Brian's mam ushered him out of the car. Brian blatantly said that he didn't know who they were. I just sniggered. I thought it was hilarious that Brian was trying to deny knowing them, especially since both the grandmother and the children had recognised him. Brian's mam told him that he had been caught out and that he couldn't lie his way out of this one. We left and went back to the cottage. We argued when we got home and Brian's mam stood in my defence. Even after everything, Brian carried on denying it.

Brian's mam often called to the house to see if we were OK, as she adored her new grandson. However, I sometimes found that the Kenny family was around us too much. Some days I felt that their presence could be overpowering. It often felt that it was not a relationship between Brian and me, but more like one that was between me and the Kenny family. After returning from Brian's mistress's house and arguing, eventually Brian's mam went home and Brian left the house at the same time. So, again I was alone. I was hurt and humiliated once again. I was numb and very sad and could not speak.

Brian arrived home that evening, still in denial, but he was apologising. He remained adamant that he had not had any involvement with the woman, even though I had the evidence. When I pointed out that fact to him, he immediately became aggressive and abusive towards me. He began by pulling at my clothing and at my hair. He slapped me around the head and then pushed me onto the sofa. Each time that I tried to get up he pushed me down. That was Brian's intention – to keep me down. I remember getting up to try to stop him and then I felt his fist in my face. I gave up. I will never forget that night. Once again I had confronted him and he had reacted as he usually did, leaving me with two black eyes and a broken heart.

The following day Brian's father visited the house. He was shocked when he saw the state I was in. Brian was missing and nowhere to be found. Later that day Brian's two sisters called to the house and sat in the living room staring at me. I was embarrassed and I cried. They were disgusted with Brian. I remember saying that I wished that I had never come off life support, as my life had become such hell. I don't remember his sisters asking me about the attacks again. Brian's violence and the beatings he gave me were never mentioned. Maybe they were in denial and just didn't want to think about what their brother was doing to me.

I am sure that some people will wonder why on earth I remained with Brian after that. Really I was fighting my own battle with my health, so much so that I couldn't face another one. I forgave him. I had been sick for so long that I thought that maybe I had forced him into another woman's arms.

I never would have had Brian down as a womaniser. If indeed he was good at wooing other women, he was good at hiding it from me. I had never seen him flirt or hit on other women in front of me. I later read that as a drug dealer, he would accept sex in exchange for drugs. He really preyed on other people's misery. On one occasion, Brian had offered an addict drugs in return for sex with one of his young sidekicks, which the young lad declined. It makes me sick now to even think that I once shared a bed with this animal.

Life for me at the cottage was very lonely, even though

there was a constant flow of people through the house with Brian's popularity continuing to grow. I spent most of my evenings enjoying my pastime, which was painting. I loved to buy blank canvasses, oils and acrylics, and let my mind in someway escape this madness. I would spend hours on my creations. I always felt relaxed and at ease when I had finished one. It was my way of switching off and dissociating myself from the situation that I was in.

Brian was becoming more aggressive and violent towards me. I was receiving beatings for no apparent reason – not that there is any valid reason to carry out a beating on any woman. He returned home one day when I was in the kitchen doing some washing. When he came in through the back door, he locked it without saying a word. He grabbed me by the hair and swung me and dragged me around the kitchen. Then he took the metal sweeping brush in his hand and beat me with it until it bent in the middle. I remember that I tried to call my sister on the house phone when he had left the room, but when Brian heard me he pulled it from the wall, removed it from the kitchen and left the house. My sister Mary rang the gardaí, but they never came.

Mary tried her best to encourage me to leave Brian. She despised him and she could see him for what he really was.

That year Brian's parents moved away from their home on Collin's Avenue in Whitehall and bought a house in Drogheda, Co. Louth. Brian's mam felt disgraced by the family's involvement with drugs, but the disgrace would follow them. Brian was not finished with earning his fortune in whatever way possible.

The Kenny family was closely-knit, and many weekends we would visit them in their new house in Drogheda. Brian seemed to have a way of ruling the roost there. He was the eldest and seemed to have some kind of hold over them. He could always set the mood in the house. Everyone seemed to have to humour him. It seemed like everyone was trying to avoid any trouble or quarrels. He also enjoyed humiliating me and putting me down in front of everyone. There was one quote that he used quite frequently when he was insulting me: 'I took you out of the gutter and I will put you back in the gutter where I found you.'

Brian thought that he was someone special and that I wasn't good enough for him. I knew otherwise, and I did not hold his opinion in high regard at that stage. He thought the more money you had, the better a person you were. He had no moral fibre, and respected nothing more than money and wealth. Brian would explore any avenue open to him in his quest for cash. When we visited

Brian's parents we would often go to the Morning Star pub in Drogheda, and enjoy the céilí nights there. I would spend the evening enjoying the dancing and music, while Brian would spend most of the evening on the poker machines at the back of the bar. It was an addictive habit that Brian shared with his father. They won sometimes, but not very often. Sometimes I would accompany Brian to another gambling venue off the Drumcondra Road. I also remember Brian bringing Joey to Caesar's Palace on Doyle's Corner. Brian gambled quite a lot back then. He would often get quite frustrated and agitated when he lost. He could not enjoy the simpler things in life like art, music or nature, as most people do. For Brian, everything had to have an edge. Gambling was just another way that Brian thought he could make his fortune.

It was now 1999 and Conor was about two years of age. At that time Brian had befriended a young man called Seamus. Seamus was a member of the travelling community. Brian would go out with him and collect copper from anywhere they could. I liked Seamus. He was inoffensive, smart, well dressed and a very good-looking young man. His wife was always with him when he called to the house. They were a very civil and loving couple. Copper was another way for Brian to make money and Seamus was teaching him how to sell it. Whether it was done illegally or not I don't know.

Things were now really bad between us. Brian would often lock me into the house with the kids. Seamus would sometimes arrive to find Brian not at home. When he saw that I was actually locked into the house, Seamus would stand there in disbelief shaking his head. He would ask me if I needed anything from the shops and so on. Seamus could not get his head around Brian's actions. I would often give him money through the tiny window and he would gladly go to the garage up the road. I'm sure he wondered why I didn't smash a window to get out, but he was unaware of the price I would have to pay for doing that. Seamus had no idea that Brian was as violent as he was. I couldn't smash the window in case the broken glass would have been used on me.

Brian didn't get on with one of Seamus' brothers. I am not sure why. Maybe it was because the brother did not agree with the business arrangement that Brian and Seamus had together. I know that the brother didn't like Brian either. Seamus' brother was not as placid as Seamus was. If Brian was ever in the same company as him there would be a tense atmosphere and taunting looks between the pair.

Sadly that year Seamus passed away. He had been out with his wife and son, driving around looking for copper.

He got out of his van on a building site and went to investigate the yard. To his wife and child's horror a very large cement-block wall collapsed and crushed him. I believe that his wife and child ran to his side. His last words to her were of love and concern. He asked her to take the child away as he did not want his son to see his father die like that. He then took his last breath and sadly passed away.

A year later, on Seamus' anniversary, Brian and I were in bed. I was just dozing off to sleep when I heard an enormous crash. We both jumped out of bed. I was screaming as Conor was in the front bedroom that faced onto the main road. The noise seemed to be coming from that direction. We could hear banging and crashing of glass. When we opened the bedroom door, we could see the windows were all coming in. We had no idea what or who was smashing them. I ran to get Conor from his cot. To my absolute horror I found him in the cot screaming with glass and rocks around him. Thank God Conor was not injured. It is a miracle that he didn't get any cuts, especially with the amount of glass and rocks in his cot.

Brian ran out of the house to see what had happened. He got dressed and went out in the car to see if he could catch up with the perpetrators on the road. He managed to catch them, only to discover that it was Seamus' brother. He had been out drinking, drowning his sorrows on Seamus' anniversay. Obviously his hatred for Brian was still festering, and he had taken that hate out by breaking every window at the front of the cottage that night.

We stayed awake for the remainder of the night. Brian tried to patch up the windows, but it was no use. We called a glazier the next morning to repair the windows. Before they were repaired, Brian went to the halting site where the family lived and returned with Seamus' parents. He wanted to show them what their son had done. Brian demanded payment for the damage. The parents argued that they were not happy about that. I brought the mother to the window at the front of the house and told her to look inside. She was horrified when she saw the cot. She apologised for what her son had done. They both feared retaliation over the attack on our home. It never happened – at least I don't think so. Things settled down and I heard no more about it. I didn't see any of Seamus' family again after that night. Life at Mitchelstown Cottage was getting extremely dangerous. Brian's notoriety was increasing, for all the wrong reasons.

Time went on and Brian decided to build a shed at the back of the house. The man that was building it was terribly nice and quiet, and it was good to have his company every day. George was his name. While George was there doing the work, I was happy, as it was keeping Brian away from me. I was sorry when he finished the shed, as I knew the abuse would start again.

Brian had started bringing Joey home with him each day after they had finished the milk round. Joey was a nice kid. I was very fond of him. He was with Brian a lot. Joey had also been helping Brian and George to build the shed. I was worried though. Brian was not a good role model and I felt he was a bad influence on Joey. I didn't want Joey to become one of Brian's sidekicks. Unfortunately, Brian would eventually use Joey as his lackey.

Joey had lived in Ballymun in his younger years until his family moved to Blakestown. He was one of five children. Joey had witnessed violence early on in his young life at the hands of his mam's ex-partner. The violence was not only used on his mam, but also on Joey. I think that this violence led to Joey's troubled teenage years. Sometimes he could be an angry young man, but most of the time he was loving and affectionate. He was never afraid to give me a hug or to be affectionate with the kids. Later on when he gradually moved into our lives, and was living with us on a permanent basis, I noticed how childish he could sometimes be. Joey was not the big man that he thought he was when he was around Brian. He was very impressionable and wanted to please people.

I think Joey thought Brian was invincible. The poor lad soon discovered that Brian was not invincible – he just didn't care about the consequences of his actions. He loved to be cared for, and was like a child when you made a fuss of him. I would often throw the duvet over him if he had fallen asleep on the couch, and he was happy that you cared enough to do that for him. When I look back I realise that Joey and I had both lost our fathers at a young age. We were both vulnerable. I think Brian preyed on our vulnerability. If either of our father's had been alive Brian would not have got away with what he did to us.

ꕥ

I was still attending the hospital for regular check-ups for my gallbladder. The doctors had told me that I may need more surgery to have my gallbladder removed. I had been in excruciating pain. The doctor told me that there could be numerous gallstones. He said that it was not uncommon for a woman who has previously had a hysterectomy to find that she also needs to have her gallbladder removed. There is a wall of muscle that divides these two organs and once one of them has been removed the other one weakens, causing problems for the patient and necessitating further surgery. The thought of going back to hospital didn't appeal to me, but I was in so much pain I knew it was inevitable.

I had another appointment that week in St Vincent's. However, during that week Brian was abusive again. On one occasion he threw the microwave out the patio door – it smashed into pieces on the ground. I was clearing it up when my brother Joe arrived to visit. When Joe saw what had happened he immediately wanted to go into the house and confront Brian, but I wouldn't let him. I knew too well that Brian would try to have Joe done for trespassing and assault. Joe was trying to protect me, but I knew at the time that if he went in and confronted Brian it would only make things worse.

I decided to leave Brian that week. My sister came to the house and gathered my belongings and some of the kids' things. We went and stayed in Mary's house. The following morning, Mary accompanied me to the hospital for my appointment. We were sitting in the waiting area when Brian came through the door, hurling abuse at us. I was mortified. He demanded to know were his son was. We told him that Mary's daughter, Emma, was minding him. He left. I saw the doctor and he gave me the date of my operation.

On the way home Emma called. She was hysterical

on the phone. Brian was at her house and was trying to break in. Mary alerted a neighbour, and the gardaí came. Brian was cautioned and left. Again he was getting off lightly. I, on the other hand, was worried about what he might do to my sister and her family. I was so worried about their safety and getting them involved in my problems that I returned to Mitchelstown Cottage that night, much to my sister's dismay. Mary had pleaded with me not to, but I didn't want to put her through any further hassle or harassment from Brian. I felt so bad that both Emma and Mary had been affected by Brian and his violent outbursts.

I had settled back in at the cottage and was trying to bring some normality to my life. That wasn't easy while living with Brian. I knew that life would never be normal as long as I stayed there with him. At the time I was just trying to survive and keep my family together, which meant keeping my head down and tyring to not get Brian annoyed. Brian continued to steal and he continued to attract a number of undesirables. I do not know where or how Brian managed to get to know these people.

Joey was also still hanging around too much and I worried about him. He was a good kid but he was young and he appeared to really want to please Brian. It seemed like he craved a father figure. Unfortunately, he picked someone who only cared about himself to fill that role. Brian would shape and mould Joey into what he wanted him to be, as he had done to me. Joey would soon be under Brian's control, and once Brian had him, there would be no getting away without a fight. Brian would ruin this young man's life. Forever. Brian was a control freak who used violence to empower himself. Poor Joey was soon going to discover that.

On another occasion, I had been out in the car with Brian. When we got back to the house and the car had come to a stop in the driveway, Brian got out and opened the shed doors so that he could park the car inside. It was not unusual for him to do that, so I remained in the car until it had reached its final parking spot. When Brian had parked the car inside the shed, I got out but before I could head for the cottage, Brian locked the front and side doors of the shed. He then took a plank of wood and began to beat me with it. I was crying and begging him to stop and tried to take cover behind whatever I could. At some stage I must have cried out my father's name. Brian responded by yelling: 'There's no use calling your Da now. He can't help ya!'

The beating went on for about twenty minutes, until Brian had eventually pleasured himself enough by controlling me, and gave up. He then went into the cottage to watch television as if nothing had happened. I stayed in the shed, crying and trying to understand what had just occurred. I went into the kitchen and made a cup of tea to try to calm myself, while drawing hard on a cigarette. I was shaking violently and I inspected my body for bruises. I didn't call the police, as I did not see the point. I didn't think they would come, because they hadn't come before when I called them. This random act of violence was not unusual for Brian.

No matter how many times Brian attacked me or whatever pain he had put me through I never understood why he did it. My body had been through enough due to bad health and it was now taking a battering from him. This was a person that at one point I had loved, and I could not understand how on earth he could put me through this life of hell. I had had a sheltered childhood and I had never experienced any form of violence in my life. I really didn't know what way to deal with it and I felt ashamed.

I was raised well by my parents. We were raised with values and morals. We were always taught that it was wrong to hurt anyone else. I went through my life looking for only the good in people. I couldn't fathom how Brian could be so cruel to me. I will never understand how someone can do that to another human being. It scares me to think like that. What sick pleasure can anyone get from this behaviour? I used to try so hard to understand why Brian would torture me like this. I thought about other women that may be going through the same abuse and wondered how they were handling it. I had gone through life unharmed by any human being. My parents did not believe in using any form of violence towards us when we were growing up. My dad believed that it was better to sit with a child and explain to them what they had done wrong and what had resulted from their actions by pointing out the consequences. This is how I deal with my own children.

*

Even though I was still apprehensive about remaining in the relationship with Brian, I was also feeling apprehensive about the looming surgery. I was petrified and thought of little else. Past experiences haunted me and I worried about possible complications. I was admitted to St Vincent's and underwent surgery to have my gallbladder removed. I stayed in hospital for three days. I had the operation by keyhole surgery, which meant that I had no open wounds this time, thankfully. It would make it easier for me to cope at home with Conor. He was heading for his first birthday, and not yet walking, which meant that I was still lifting and carrying him.

On the evening that I came home from hospital, my brother Joe arrived at the house to see me. We sat and chatted and Brian joined in. Later that evening Joe and Brian decided to go for a couple of pints in the local pub, Dolly Heffernan's, which was about a quarter of a mile to the rear of the cottage. If Joe had known what was really going on with Brian, I have no doubt he wouldn't have gone out for drinks with him. The night was closing in and there was no sign of them returning, so I decided to go to bed as I was tired and and still sore from the operation.

Later that night I woke up to find Brian standing over me, he was digging my arm with his fist, trying to wake me up. I sat up in the bed and asked him what was wrong. I gazed at the clock and saw that it was 4.00 a.m. Brian closed and locked the door. He told me to stand in the corner. I was still half asleep and confused. He again told me to stand in the corner. I refused and lay back down. Then he dragged me by the hair and pulled me from the bed, demanding that I stand in the corner. I knew what was about to happen. He launched into an attack and punched and kicked me so much that I grew too tired to fight him off. I was on the floor, curled up in the foetal position. He was above me kicking and digging my delicate body. I was crying and begging him to stop, but he wouldn't. I was afraid that Robyn would hear and come to her mam's aid and be the recipient of one of his blows.

He was like a madman. He lifted me up by the back of my neck and threw me onto the bed. Then he tried to strangle me. I could feel my airways blocked and my face was filled with blood from the pressure. My eyes were bulging from their sockets. Then he let go, leaving me gasping for air.

After he released me, Brian calmly undressed and got into bed. I fled the room. I sat on the sofa for hours, crying, not knowing what to do. I checked on the kids and they were fine. I thought: *why had he done that? What will I do? If I call the gardaí, will they come? If I call them, what will he do?* All of these questions went through my mind until I convinced myself not to call them. I should have, but I didn't. I was too afraid. I should have been stronger, but I was too weak to fight and my heart was hurting. I was still exhausted from being in hospital and was recovering from the operation. I knew that someday I would leave Brian and Mitchelstown Cottage, but I would need a plan. I would need to have a place to escape to. I would need some money of my own and I would have to find somewhere safe to stay.

I later found out from my brother Joe that he had left Brian at around midnight that night. I guessed that Brian had gone offside afterwards to score some type of drug before he came home and attacked me.

My family was unaware of the extent of Brian's behaviour. I kept a lot hidden from them. In some ways I was ashamed that I had chosen him as a partner. I especially kept a lot hidden from my brother as I was afraid that he would intervene on my behalf. I did not want him to get himself into trouble because of me and because of my choices. I knew that Joe would have done his utmost to help me if he had known the full extent of Brian's brutality. As time went on, it became more obvious to people what was going on in our relationship. Things changed and people began to get angry when they realised what Brian was doing to me. My brother tried to help, and I know that some of his friends had threatened Brian and told him to keep his hands off me. Threats did not bother Brian and he still carried on attacking me.

I had never before witnessed or experienced the disrespect and violence that I received from Brian. I had never heard my father raise his voice to my mother. Any male figures in my life had always been respectfull and honourable. I was so shocked that I did not know how to react, or, more importantly, how to deal with it.

At the beginning of our relationship my family liked Brian to a degree. Although, maybe they were just saying that because I seemed happy. Joe said that he liked him in the beginning, but as time went on all their views changed. Mary despised him, and to this day she cannot even mention his name. She even finds it hard to have a conversation about him.

Months passed and I was still living in this hell. Brian took more and more pleasure in brutalising me and tormenting me in any way possible. He would lock me in the house and lock me out of the house. He'd take my mobile phone (sometimes smashing it), my house key, car keys, the house phone, even the kettle so I couldn't make a cup of tea.

Brian even cut my clothes off one night as I got ready to meet my pals Karen and Martina for a drink. I had not seen them for sometime, and I would not let them visit me there. I had told them what Brian was up to, and didn't want them coming to the cottage. I preferred to go out and meet them so that I didn't have to worry about Brian coming back at any minute. They had seen the bald patches on my head that Brian had left after yanking my hair out.

It was not very often that I got to see my friends. If I saw them once every six months I was lucky. If I told Brian that I had arranged to meet them, I always worried about what his reaction would be. He always caused a big fuss and commotion when I told him, so, often, it just didn't seem worth it. He did not like the relationship that I had with my friends and I think that he thought that they posed some type of threat to him, plus he knew that they really disliked him.

I had arranged to meet Karen and Martina for drinks that evening. We were to meet at Karen's house at 8.30 p.m. I was looking forward to catching up with them, hearing all the latest gossip and having a giggle. Brian was to babysit the kids while I went out, which was going to cause another problem. Brian didn't like doing things because he had to, he only liked to do things because he wanted to.

That evening I got ready: I showered, dressed, blow-dried my hair and applied my make-up. I was delighted to be going out, but I was also nervous. I was nervous of an argument erupting before I went out, and worried about a possible argument when I came home. As I got ready,

Brian lay on the sofa watching TV. He said nothing and his silence was really worrying me. I knew something was brewing. When I was ready I told him that I was going to call a cab and then I looked for my mobile phone, which I couldn't find. Alarm bells rang in my head and I suspected that he had hidden it. When I told him that I couldn't find it, and that I would have to use the house phone to call the cab, things spiralled out of control.

Brian marched from the livingroom to the kitchen and pulled the house phone from the wall socket. He wrapping the cord around the phone and shoved it into a press under the TV. I didn't dare try to retrieve it as I knew what the consequences would be. I just calmly sat on the sofa facing him and asked him why he was doing what he was doing. He had known for weeks in advance that I was going to meet my friends. I begged him to call me a cab, but he refused. It was nearly 9.00 p.m. and I knew that the girls would be wondering where I was. Then I heard the tone of my mobile phone ringing; it was coming from Brian's direction. Realising that my intuition was right and that Brian had in fact taken my phone, I got annoyed and stood above him demanding that he give it back to me. I was getting frustrated because I knew that it was Karen calling, wondering where I was. I kept demanding that

Brian give me back the phone so I could take Karen's call. Brian jumped up from the sofa and growled at me that I was not going out. The violence started and he pushed and pulled me around the room.

I escaped into the bedroom and waited to see if he would calm down. He didn't. He came through the bedroom door with a large scissors in his hand. I was so scared. Sheer panic shot through me. I had no idea what he was about to do. He grabbed me and cut through my clothes until they were in ribbons on the floor. He left the room and I sat on the bed and cried.

A few minutes later Brian reappeared in the doorway and said that he was sorry. I couldn't even look at him. He came and sat on the bed beside me and put his arm around me and kept saying that he was sorry. He told me to get ready and go and meet my friends and that he would say no more about it. I remained sitting on the bed until I heard my mobile phone ring again, so I decided to take my chances and get ready to meet my friends. Brian said no more as I got ready and left the house.

When I eventually got to Karen's house, it was nearly 10.00 p.m. Both Karen and Martina had been waiting patiently for me. They had arranged to meet some of their cousins in a pub on Hanlon's Corner in Cabra. The rest of the evening went well; we all shared a few drinks and a few laughs.

It was nearly closing time and we had just ordered our last drinks of the evening when I noticed that Martina was looking at me with shock written all over her face. I was confused and saw that she was signalling me to look in the direction of the door. When I looked through the circular window, I could see Brian staring back at me. He did not acknowledge me or wave to say hello. He just stared at me and he did not look happy. It was so strange and disconcerting. I stayed in my seat. Karen and Martina were agitated by Brian's sudden appearance. They were really worried about me. It was a really freaky thing to do.

We wondered how long Brian had actually been standing there watching me. We decided to finish our drinks, and we all made our way onto the street, where we would hopefully find a cab to take us home. When we left the building, I immediately heard Brian's voice calling me. Karen linked my arm, and guided me away from him. He had been sitting outside in a jeep with his friend Peter Joyce. God only knows how long they had been there. I had no idea why he was there or what his intention was. I had told the girls just how hard it had been for me to get out of the house that night. Seeing Brian had put them all on the defensive. It was obvious that he was trying to freak me out. It just emphasised to me and to them how controlling his behaviour had become.

Karen's cousin was feisty. She marched up to Brian and told him to leave the area and to leave me alone. I was grateful for their concern, and for Karen's cousin's reaction. I thought to myself there is going to be World War III when I get home. Then I became even more alarmed when I realised that Brian was supposed to be babysitting. If he was here, who was looking after my children? Karen's cousin and Brian were screaming abuse at one another. Peter Joyce did not get involved. He just watched. Karen hailed a cab and Martina and I piled in with her. They both knew that I was really worried about the kids, so they dropped me home first. When I got into the cottage I found my niece Emma there.

I thanked God that the kids were not alone. However, Emma told me that she was there under protest. Brian had gone looking for Emma late that night. He found her with a group of teenage friends close to where she lived. Brian asked her to babysit, but she had refused. She said that Brian told her that she had to and demanded that she got in the car. Now he was bullying my family members. I felt bad that Emma had experienced this type of bullying from Brian. She must have felt awful and must have been embarrassed that her group of friends had seen Brian speaking to her like this. I wondered who had been minding the kids while Brian went out to find Emma.

I went to bed and waited for Brian to come home. Emma stayed the night. In a strange way I found some comfort in that as I knew that Brian would not strike me in front of her. After all, it was about control and Brian would not have wanted my family to know the full extent of his hold over me. An hour or so had passed and there was no sign of Brian coming home, so I guessed that he must have stayed out with Peter Joyce. I awoke the next morning to find him in the kitchen playing with Conor. He acted like nothing strange or out of the ordinary had happened the night before.

Brian was like a ticking time bomb. A time bomb that could go off at any moment without any warning or for no reason. All day, every day you had to brace yourself for an explosion of violence, hate and pure insanity.

I had to sleep in a truck one night in my bra and knickers when he locked me out of the house. There was snow on the ground and it was freezing. The house was so isolated that I had no one to run to. Some nights I thought about boiling the kettle and pouring it over him as he slept, but I couldn't do that – although the thought was nice.

I often woke up in the middle of the night to find Brian straddling me. He tried to suffocate me with pillows. He would push down hard on my face, and I would try wrestling from beneath, gasping for air, until he would give up, for whatever reason. I don't know why he did this. It just made me think that he was a psychopath.

On one occasion, I decided to get Robyn to photograph my damaged and bruised body. I had purchased a disposable camera. I wanted photographic evidence of what he had done and what he was putting me through. It must have been awful for my daughter to have to take those photos of her mother. Robyn photographed my back, arms and legs. I also photographed the piles of my blonde hair that he had yanked out. I put the clumps of hair on the black marble fireplace so that they could be seen more clearly in the photograph. I had the photos developed and hid them away in books. I had obviously thought about having him prosecuted at a later stage, and thought that these photos would have provided some evidence.

Around this time I attended one of the women's refuge centres. I made my visit there as quickly and as secretively as I could. I had read a lot of women's reviews on these centres. They all seemed to have had positive experiences. Unfortunately, I did not. I left the centre clueless. I spoke to a woman for about half an hour or so, explaining my situation to her. It was like a counselling session, where I poured out all of my heartache and pain. I was like a child looking for a plaster to be placed on a scratch, making it better so that the pain would go away. I thought that this woman was going to give me an instant solution to my problem. The more that I spoke to her, the more I could hear myself describing my life as it was at that moment, and I hated myself for being in that situation and for being me. However, after talking to her, I left the refuge centre and went back to the cottage – back to my nightmare situation. I was afraid, and prayed that Brian had not discovered my visit. I never went back to the centre; at the time I was too afraid he would find out. I was also afraid that he would see my cry for help as his victory and think that he had succeeded in breaking me.

Chapter Four

The Sunday Drive

The mood in the house was always set by Brian's Dr Jekyll and Mr Hyde personality. You never knew what to expect from him – each day was different than the last. If he was happy you were thankful that you were going to have a good day. But his happy days were few and far between. The kids and I were happy when he was not at home. We carried on as any other normal household would, until we heard the key in the lock and the slide of the patio door. Then we jumped to attention as if preparing for defence. I would feel myself get anxious. My heart would race and I would draw deep breaths while I waited to see which way I would be greeted.

Brian started picking on me one day and I was feeling worn out by his persistent barrage of verbal abuse, as he moved around the house banging and breaking anything that got in his way. I knew that the level of abuse could escalate into something more violent, so I made a run for it before it peaked. I made my way out to the car and strapped Conor in the back, while Robyn climbed in beside her brother. I started the engine and reversed out of the drive. I had no idea where I was going. Brian heard the engine and I could see his face through the living room window. He dashed out the front door. I could see him in the rear view mirror as he chased after the car along the road. I don't know how, but he caught up with me and pounced onto the car holding on to the sunroof, which was open. It was like something that you would see in a Hollywood film. It was like he was possessed.

Brian was so determined to get the better of me that he would go to any lengths, even if it meant sprinting down the road, chasing a moving car and jumping onto it. He kept shouting at me through the windscreen to stop the car. I wouldn't. I kept my foot on the excelerator and continued down the road. My visibility was bad, as Brian's frame was blocking my view, his body sprawled across my windscreen. He was swaying from side to side. The kids were remarkably quiet in the back – I think they were in shock. An odd time Robyn let out a disbelieving: 'Oh

Mam!' I just told her that it was OK. I continued driving in the hope that Brian would fall off at some point. He didn't. Somehow he was able to pull his body upwards, and as I continued to drive, he managed to get himself through the sunroof. I turned to find him sitting beside me laughing. I continued driving. I was still in shock at what he had just done.

He asked me where I was going. I told him I was going to Finglas garda station. He was laughing hysterically now, which made me more determined to reach my destination. When we arrived at the garda station, I got out of the car. I told him to get out and follow me in. I asked him if he would prefer if I brought the gardaí out to him. He was still laughing uncontrollably and just refused point blank. He was quick to point out that he had done nothing and that I had no bruises to show the gardaí. He said that I was wasting my time going in there, as they would only laugh at me. I thought about it for a few minutes before I got back into the car and made my way home. He had called my bluff. I should have seen it through.

Brian had many ways of intimidating us and using us. One of the things he loved to do was take us out on a Sunday drive. He would pack us all into the car and head off in a random direction. We hated it. We dreaded 'The

Sunday Drive'. Really what Brian was doing was using us as a front: the happy family out for a drive. He was in fact staking out premises, which he later would possibly burgle.

I often found myself abandoned in the middle of nowhere because Brian had thrown me out of the car. He would throw me out because I objected to what he was doing. It was also another way for him to mentally abuse me. He loved playing games and this was just another sick way to mess with my head and make him feel in control. Then he would drive away with the kids in the car, and leave me to walk for miles before returning for me.

On one occasion I remember he abandoned me in the middle of the countryside, somewhere close to Mullingar, in Westmeath. He sped off and left me walking in the direction that we had come from. I was nervous wandering the country lanes, as the landscape seemed barren and lonely. I had no way of contacting anyone for help and I had no money to get a bus or a train. I just prayed that he would return for me. He didn't always come back, so I never knew how long it would take me to get home to the kids.

Once he threw me out of the car at the bottom of Bay Lane. He leaned across me and opened the door. He then lifted his feet up from the pedals and kicked me out of the car. I fell into a ditch. I had to walk the rest of the way home to find that, once more, I was locked out as he sat in the living room, laughing out the window at me. The kids sat there with frightened looks on their little faces. Even though it was only a twenty-minute walk, it felt like miles.

By this stage Robyn despised him. I could see it in her eyes. It was heartbreaking. But I didn't blame her; I felt the same way. Why wouldn't she hate a man, who she had once considered a father figure, after seeing all the things he had done to her family? For someone so young, Robyn had witnessed so much violence and abuse: mental, physical and psychological. He was an evil monster, one sick bastard. Every time Brian went out at night I prayed to God that he would be caught.

ꕥ ꕥ

Conor's first birthday had gone by, and the year seemed to have passed me by quite quickly. Before I knew it, we were into the New Year. The weather was cold and the dark nights were long. My health was improving and I was feeling a lot stronger. It was 2000: the millennium. There had been some changes in Kilshane that year. The cottage adjacent to ours had been renovated and we had new neighbours. The kennels at the back of the cottage stood on about an acre of land. The owner had built a bungalow on the land and was going to live there permanently. They were good neighbours, although I didn't get to spend a lot of time with them. I knew that they sympathised with me. They couldn't but have been aware of the beatings that Brian was giving me. Betty, the lady that lived in the bungalow attached to the kennels, had witnessed the abuse first hand. She had tried to stop Brian from drowning me in the paddling pool the previous summer. On another occasion, she was alerted by Robyn crying in the back garden and came to investigate. She found Brian holding me in a headlock and twisting my arms behind my back.

Caroline, the woman next door, didn't take any crap from Brian. He tried his best to antagonise her but she wasn't afraid of him. Whenever she had an issue with Brian she would confront him. There were a few arguments between the two of them. I also argued with her occasionally, even though I knew that Brian was in the wrong. Really all I wanted her to do was go, so that the argument was not carried back into the cottage – where I would have to take the brunt of it.

He started a lot of arguments with the neighbours, making it harder for me to have contact or to build friendships with them. That made his job a whole lot easier.

He could continue battering me, knowing too well that I would not run to them. It was another way to keep me isolated and to ensure I didn't have support close by.

Brian also tried to terrorise Aidan, who was the owner of the kennels. Aidan was not afraid of Brian, and there were often cross words between the two men. The two of them had been friends in the beginning. Brian and I had often gone for a drink with him at the weekends. I liked Aidan. I could understand exactly where his hate for Brian came from. After they fell out, Aidan had to purchase a security dog. The security dog wandered around the grounds of the kennels patrolling them at nightime. Aidan got the security dog because of the threats that Brian had made against his business. Aidan did not trust Brian and he was right not to.

I could see a pattern forming with Brian – he never seemed to be able to sustain friendships. Every friend that he ever made while we were together always fell by the wayside. The friendships never lasted because Brian would have destroyed them in some cruel way. Brian destroyed everything that he came in contact with. He lost interest in things and people very quickly. I often wondered how his mind worked. Some days you would be having a perfectly normal conversation with Brian, and as you looked into his eyes at times it seemed that someone had turned a switch on and he would become a completely different person. He would become hostile and dismissive. The physical change in his face would always be obvious. When this happened you automatically knew at that moment to say no more.

Since leaving Kilshane, I have visited my former neighbour, Caroline, on a couple of occasions. We chatted and remembered the old days. Caroline told me that she used to feel sorry for me when she heard Brian battering me. She said she could hear the commotion through the adjoining walls. Unfortunately, she was powerless to do anything.

By that time Brian had broken me and robbed me of my smile. I felt that I had lost my soul. I was no longer the happy-go-lucky Rita. I was an emotional wreck left with no optimism and no prospects of fulfilment or happiness. I felt trapped. Inside I was screaming. It's a very, very scary place to be. I was so exhausted as I tried to cope with my emotions and deal with my situation. When you feel like that, you feel like your brain just wants to shut down so that the mental anguish will go away. You try to understand why this is happening to you and what it is that you have done wrong. You begin to dislike yourself for turning into this submissive weak woman. You don't trust yourself to make decisions about anything, especially when you feel that you must have had the poor judgement to choose such a violent partner. How could I trust myself now with anything?

Chapter Five

The Tony Soprano of Finglas

Brian was still collecting pallets and young Joey was helping him. I became very fond of him and so did the kids. He would play with Robyn and rough house with Conor on the floor. We called Joey, 'Joey the Lips', because he had huge rosey-red lips that any girl would die for. Joey would get really embarrassed when we jeered him about it. He was such a good-looking kid, and was always immaculately dressed.

I always told Joey that if Brian ever asked him to do anything that he thought was wrong that he should say no and that I would back him up. Brian was getting increasingly out of control – thieving all around him. I knew that he would pressure Joey into doing something against the law. I didn't want Joey staying at the house. It was all right for a while, as Joey's dad had recently passed away, and Brian seemed to be company for him. Young Joey had a lovely family. His mam was a pleasant woman, and his sisters were always happy and very polite. However, I knew that Joey was not getting on well with his brother, and sometimes there would be a tricky situation at home. It seemed to be typical stuff that brothers fought and argued about. I know that Joey would not have wanted to stay at the house had he known what Brian was capable of. Poor Joey; if he had known what the future held, he would have run a mile.

On one occasion, Brian told me that he was bringing Joey with him on a job. He was planning to steal a cherry picker from a premises on the North Road. When I went mad and told him not to do it, Brian pushed me and backed me into a corner between the bathroom and the attic stairs. With one hand he lifted me and slid me up the wall by the throat as I struggled for air. Joey tried to help and begged Brian to stop. With just one punch Brian sent Joey flying across the hallway. When Brain eventually relented, both Joey and I were crying. He was just a kid. I sat on the bed with Joey and tried to comfort him. I cradled him, as he sobbed like a baby. It didn't seem to bother Brian that Joey had not only witnessed my attack, but had suffered as a result. There were many times that

Joey and I stood up for each another. There were many times that we found ourselves pacifying Brian and agreeing with him when we feared that he was getting angry. We both knew what Brian was capable of. We both knew how important it was to try to prevent him going off on one.

After that attack, Brian didn't stop and continued to use Joey to help with his activities. I remember he set out late one night with Joey. It was a dark, dark night and it was pouring down. I had no idea where they were going. A few hours later they arrived home with a boat hitched up to the tow bar on the back of Brian's van. It just proved that nothing was safe. It wasn't an expensive boat; it looked more like one of those tug boats that you see in the movies guiding the larger ships into harbour. That week, Brian and Joey set about painting the boat to disguise it. Brian then had the boat moored in Drogheda. He used it occasionally to sail off Clogherhead in County Louth.

I was growing more anxious as I witnessed young Joey's participation in Brian's criminal activity. In a way I think that Joey was enjoying the excitement and the element of danger. In the beginning I think it seemed like fun to him. But I was also sure that Brian bullied him along the way, and, because Joey was so young, he probably would have been afraid to say no to him. I remember having a few arguments with Brian about Joey and I remember demanding that Joey return to his family home. I was becoming more aware of the activities that Brian was involving himself and Joey in. On one occassion they had tried to steal from a garage somewhere on the North Road. The garage was closed up for the night and the owners had left. Brian opened a window to the rear of the garage. Because Joey was relatively small, Brian got him to climb inside and scour the garage for money or anything else of value. I believe that the owner returned and the two had to make a run for it.

Brian was getting Joey into a lot of sticky situations. Joey had seen Brian as a father figure in the beginning, but they had become friends and partners in crime. Joey couldn't see how Brian was manipulating him or how the petty crimes they committed would escalate.

Brian was also getting deeper into things that I was not fully aware of. He had become involved with two brothers who were known to the gardaí and who were classified as being career criminals. The two had been at the house on several occasions, and I knew that Brian was involved in some way with them. I was losing track of all the comings and goings at the cottage. There was more and more activity at the house, and there was a constant flow of stolen property being shifted in and out of the shed.

One evening a white truck similar to Brian's reversed into the garden. I automatically thought that it was Brian and went back to watching the television. I could hear several voices outside in the yard and went to the kitchen window to see what all the commotion was. I could see Brian and a group of guys offloading pallets of bottles of whiskey and brandy onto the forecourt. Some of them fell and smashed. I could hear them all laugh. I put the outside light on to have a better look and Brian quickly signalled for me to turn it off. I had seen enough.

A few minutes later, I saw flashing blue lights and then heard more glass smashing. I went to the window and saw garda cars on the road. People scattered everywhere. I heard a bang on the kitchen door. It was a young garda beckoning me to open the door. When I opened the door, he asked if anyone had come through the house. No one had. but he searched anyway.

A while later four detectives came into the kitchen. They questioned me for a long time. I thought, *if only they had been quicker to respond when I was being beaten in the past.* They fired questions at me from every angle; questions that I couldn't answer. They stayed for a few hours and waited to see if Brian would come home. He didn't.

One of the detectives pointed out the significance of the length of time that I had lived at Mitchelstown Cottage. He told me that I was Brian's common-law wife and was entitled to half the property as I had lived there for over four years, but that also made me responsible for half the blame for the theft of the stolen goods on the forecourt. I was terrified. I had never had any dealings with the gardaí before, other than meeting Brian's garda friend, who was a detective. They continued to question me until one of them got a phone call from another garda, who appeared to tell them to lay off me. One of the detectives said that he had been told to go easy on me as I was from a different background than the suspects.

The detectives and patrol cars left. I could see blue and white forensic tape in the garden. There was still no sign of Brian. I heard nothing more about that botched robbery either from Brian or the gardaí.

ꕤ

Brian continued stealing. He and his friends had purchased a scanning device that enabled them to tune in to the garda radio transmissions. When he was heading out on one of his missions, he would plug it into the socket in the kitchen and turn the volume up. He would leave it on the kitchen worktop, tell me to listen to it carefully and to call him on his mobile if anything came across the airwaves. When he had left the house I would turn the volume down. Leaving it in its position on the worktop, I would go and watch the television. Young Joey used to think that was hilarious. We often joked about Brian getting caught; we often prayed that he would be. Then, when we heard anyone come into the drive, we would make a dash for the kitchen. I would turn the volume back up, and both of us would take our seats at the kitchen table.

A month or so passed and Brian really had me in fear for my life because he was becoming more volatile. We were heading into Finglas one day, I can't remember what for exactly, probably for grocery shopping, when an argument erupted in the car. The kids were sitting in the back. They were scared and crying. Then Brian grabbed my hair and slammed my head into the dashboard a number of times. I tried to fend him off but he was too strong. My forehead hit the dash hard. I was lucky that he didn't break my nose. I recall another motorist's female passenger pointing in my direction as they travelled in the opposite direction towards Meath. I didn't cry. I wouldn't let him see how much pain I was in. Instead I leaned back over the seat and tried to calm the kids. I remember looking at Brian as he continued with the journey. I felt repulsed by him.

As time went on Brian was getting increasingly out of control. I remember one winter's evening it was pitch dark outside and lashing rain. I was at home with the kids and Joey when Brian came through the door like a madman. He started rummaging through the kitchen drawers and was muttering and ranting on about something or other. I had no idea what he was talking about. He handed Joey and me flashlights and he ordered us out into the dark rainy night. He marched us across the road and into the field on the other side. Both of us looked at each other curiously, not knowing what was happening. Brian then pushed me and shouted at us to to search the ditch. He told us to look for a plastic bag. It was freezing and raining heavily, and it was very hard to see. Brian pushed me further on along the ditch, ordering me to look closer. I told him that he was wasting his time and he became angry again. We both gave up our search, and I told Brian that I was heading back into the house to the kids. He was furious as we started to make our way out of the field. He continued with the search himself but came back into the house a few minutes later. He made a call on his mobile.

'It's not fucking there. I've fucking looked,' Brian growled at whoever it was on the other end of the line. 'There's eight in it. Eight. It's fucking gone!' Brian was frantic.

We were drying ourselves off with towels in the bathroom and I eavesdropped on the conversation. It became obvious that he was talking about hash; either he had left it in the field or it had been dropped there. All I knew was that Brian was now furious and I worried that I would have to bear the brunt of his fury. However, not long after that a car pulled into the drive and Brian left the house.

Brian thought that he was invincible. You could see that he craved power and notoriety. He admired notorious gangsters like Martin Cahill. He also loved *The Sopranos* and would never miss an episode. I think that Brian thought he was the Tony Soprano of Finglas – when really he was a weak little man who got off on other people's misery. He always groomed himself well. He always wore the best clothes, and boasted about his Louis Copeland or Remus Uomo shirts and suits. His body may have been clean but his mind was repulsive, sick and rotten to the core.

Joey remained living with us and brian continued to bring him out on runs with him. I was really worried for

Joey. His mam visited the house once while Brian was out. I told her that Brian was beating me, in the hope that she would take Joey out of our house, out of the violent situation. Joey had witnessed domestic violence in the past. He had witnessed his own poor mam being beaten by a violent man. I thought that she would maybe see past Brian's charming exterior. He was a fake. She thought that Brian was helping her son, when really the only one Brian was helping was himself. But I don't think she understood just how serious the situation was.

On the odd occasion that Brian and I did go out, Joey would sometimes babysit. On a couple of occasions, we went to the Harbour Bar in Balbriggin. Brian had made a few friends there and I enjoyed playing in the pool competitions. We never really could go out and say that we genuinely enjoyed ourselves. There was always a situation at the end of the night. I just went for some peace, though I rarely got it.

On one occasion an argument erupted in the car on the way home. Brian drove the car up a dirt track off the main road that led into Balbriggan. The surface of the dirt track was uneven and the car bounced as he sped along it. He brought the car to a screeching stop. He got out of the car and came around to the passenger's side. He opened the door and dragged me out. He walked further on into what seemed like a field, dragging me behind him. It was so dark that I couldn't keep my footing, and fell. He continued to drag me along the ground. Then he stopped and placed his hand under my throat. I was terrified for my life. It was pitch black and I thought there was no point in screaming for help. He took a penknife from his pocket, held it to my throat and told me that he was going to kill me. I told him to do it and put me out of my misery. His threats continued until we were disturbed by the voices of courting couples talking nearby. When he heard them, Brian pulled me up off the ground and told me to get in the car. I think I came very close to losing my life that night.

I read in Paul Williams' book that Joey said Brian had held a penknife to his throat and threatened him because he refused to babysit. I wonder was that the same night and was that the same penknife.

ꟸ ꟸ

It was coming up to 2001. The Millennium year had passed and a new year was beginning. It would be a year of change for me. I was stronger and I was angry. I was angry with myself for not getting out of this madness sooner. Another year had gone by and I was still in the cottage and still suffering in silence. Joey had left the house, and I was happy that he had got out. I spoke to him a couple of times on the phone, and he had told me that he was doing well and that he had a job. I was delighted for him. I strongly advised him to stay away from Brian and he promised me that he would.

By 2001 I had had enough of Brian. We were not sharing the same bed and the sight of him disgusted me. I knew that it would not be long before I followed in Joey's footsteps and made my escape. But I had to have a plan.

In May 2001 I began a full-time college course in Coláiste Íde in Finglas. It was a certificate in computer maintenance and upgrading. Personal development was one of the modules. I had enrolled Conor in pre-school, which allowed me to take the course. My sister Mary started the course with me. She was very supportive. I think it was her way of keeping an eye on me. If I did not show up for class one day, she would immediately know that something was wrong at the house.

I enjoyed my time on the course. I made good friends and I felt that I had accomplished a lot and come a long way. I was proud of myself and as a result I was becoming a stronger person. Brian would mock and jeer when I sat and studied in the kitchen. I suspected that he would sabotage my studies, but he didn't. He knew I was getting stronger and that I had my sister beside me.

I remember cooking dinner one day around this time. I was getting a lot of verbal abuse from Brian and I thought to myself, *any minute now* ...

I waited for the attack. I was still chopping the onions for dinner when he lunged for me. I swung around and held the carving knife to him, begging him to 'bring it on'. I could see the shock in his face. Then he just laughed and backed off. I continued making dinner, but something had changed inside me.

ꕤ

Brian's involvement in criminal activity continued throughout this time. The shed was always crammed full of stolen property. Now it was filled with stolen cars too. One evening, while I sat studying in the kitchen, I could see Brian and his mates playing music, drinking and snorting cocaine in the shed. This had become a familiar weekend occurrence for Brian. I think he was enjoying his new lifestyle. There I was studying away while he was up to no good hanging out with his dodgy friends in the shed. He was like a big teenager – a violent teenager. I was growing increasingly afraid. I didn't like the company he was keeping, but most importantly, I hated being in his company. I didn't want anything to do with him.

It was clear that Brian was interested in a new kind of criminal activity. I often heard the names Shane Coates and Stephen Suggs mentioned, and I knew that the two were known to the gardaí for drug trafficking. It was a well-known fact on the Northside that these two were trouble. I also heard Marlo Hyland being mentioned on one occasion. (All three of these men have since been murdered by gunshot.) They were all in some way knitted in to the same drug gang. I am unsure as to what exactly Brian's connection to them was.

At that time, drugs were readily available to me if I wanted them. It would be stupid and dishonest of me to say that I didn't try them. I was curious and they were there in abundance. Though I was getting stronger and was starting to get my life back on track, I was still not in a good place. Then there was the peer pressure, and the desperation that I felt also pushed me to try them. But I never really understood what exactly it was that they were supposed to do for me.

Cocaine was their drug of choice. After experimenting on few occasions, it totally lost its appeal for me. Thankfully I did not go down that road. I would have wiped away my future and my children's futures if I had. That's a scary thought. I had battled for my life after the birth of Conor and I was not about to give in and succumb to a life of drug addiction. I had my focus set firmly on the future and I knew what direction I wanted my life to take.

During that time I could see Brian's involvement with criminals increasing. He was getting into much bigger deals with harder criminals. His ego was getting bigger. Though Brian was a cold person and totally insensitive to all around him, he was enjoying the fact that his popularity with these people was increasing. I think it made him feel more powerful.

One morning I had bathed Conor and had gone to get a large bath sheet from the press over the drier in the kitchen. Conor was running around the kitchen naked and Robyn was sitting at the dining table having breakfast. When I pulled the towel down from the shelf, I could feel that it was unusually heavy. I let it go. As it fell to the ground it revealed an object that was black and brown in colour. When I opened the towel up I saw that it was a sawn-off shotgun. My heart sank. Robyn watched in disbelief. I was completely stunned. I wondered if it was loaded and was nervous picking it up. I ushered Robyn and Conor into another room. If it was loaded, it could have gone off and injured or killed one of us. I quickly wrapped the gun back up in the towel, and placed it back in the press in the exact position I found it in. I told Robyn not to say that she had seen it if Brian came home. I was relieved that Conor had not seen it. I would have to get rid of it, but how? Everything went through my head. I feared for my safety and the safety of my kids. I was afraid that Brian would use it on me if he got high enough and angry enough.

What was I going to do? I was so angry that Brian had brought a dangerous weapon into our home. It just showed me how deep his involvement in crime had become. I thought then that he really was capable of anything. If he'd threatened me with a knife, what was to stop him threatening me with a sawn-off shotgun? Then I remembered the detective that Brian had been in touch with. I had his phone number stored in my mobile. Brian had given it to me before, and asked me to call him and let him know which garda station he was being held in when he was in trouble.

I called the detective and I told him that I had found a sawn-off shotgun in my home and I wanted it removed. I didn't care how he got rid of it. I wanted it gone. He told me to calm down and then said that he would call Brian.

He said he would tell him that the house was going to be raided and he would advise Brian to remove anything he had that should not be there.

About ten minutes later Brian arrived back to the house. He rushed in through the back door and immediately ran to the press and removed the gun, before making a quick exit. I sighed with relief. To this day I don't think Brian knew about my phone call. He never mentioned it. If it had been true that the house was in fact about to be raided, Brian did nothing alert me or the kids. He just left us there like sitting ducks.

I knew that Brian was worried about his own safety. He arrived home one day with a Doberman Pinscher. He tied the dog to the rotary clothesline in the back garden. I was horrified and terrified. Brian laughed at me as I slammed the patio doors shut when the dog started to growl and bark at me ferociously. How the dog did not bite him I do not know. Maybe it was just as evil as Brian. It looked like it. I found out that Brian had stolen the dog from premises somewhere in The Ward. (The Ward is an area that runs between Kilshane and Ashbourne, in County Meath). The animal was a security dog, so I imagine that it would have attacked on command or if it came across intruders.

Brian got back into his car and left. Robyn was in

the laneway that led into the kennels behind the cottage. She was playing with her friend and I could hear the two of them laugh and giggle. Then, to my horror, the dog broke free and made a run for the lane. I ran to the fridge, grabbed a half-pound of sausages and ran out the back door. The girls screamed when they saw the dog coming at them. They both turned on their heels and ran towards the safety of the kennels. I coaxed the dog back into the garden with the sausages and tried to tie him back to the clothesline. This dog was a vicious animal and I couldn't bear to think of what it could have done to the kids if it had caught up with them.

A few minutes later a friend of Brain drove up to the cottage in his truck. I felt relieved and tried to warn him about the dog in the back garden. He was concerned about the dog. He opened the back of the truck and together we tried to coax the animal into it with whatever we could find in the fridge. When we had eventually secured the dog in the truck, he locked it up. We had a cup of tea and tried to decide what to do with it. He left with it before Brian got home. I imagine that he brought it to the pound on Scribblestown Lane.

It just proved to me once more that not only would Brian rob anything, but that he didn't give a damn about our security or safety. He was so paranoid that he went to such lengths as to get a vicious dog so he'd feel more protected. It was pure madness. It would have been too dangerous to release that dog into an uncontrolled area. When Brian returned home to find the dog missing, he wasn't happy. When I explained that it was in fact his friend that had taken the dog away from the cottage because he thought that the animal was dangerous and vicious, Brian said no more about it. Thank God Brian's friend called in that day.

Chapter Six

Educating Rita

I had completed my exams at the college and I was pleased that I had got through the course and the exams. There was a formal ceremony organised for the class to receive our awards. I had finished my course without malicious intervention from Brian – he had been kept busy with organised crime and seemed to be less interested in what I was doing. I was delighted when I saw my results and received my certificates. I had received distinctions in Computer Maintenance and Applications, and I had also completed my ECDL (European Computer Driving Licence). I was one step closer to getting the old Rita back.

It was May and we were still in the cottage. The fact that I had completed the course and passed my exams was making me feel stronger. I knew that I was preparing to eventually leave Brian.

I was disgusted one morning as Brian thought it was hysterical to watch his three-year-old son parade around the kitchen wearing a balaclava. Conor laughed along with his father, not knowing what exactly it was his father was laughing at. I laughed too – only to humour Brian. But really I was horrified. What path would Brian lead Conor down? Though I was disgusted, I didn't want a full-scale argument. I knew that I had to get my kids out of there and the sight of my son in a balaclava only strengthened my resolve.

As summer went on I was missing my classmates. Once again I was spending more time at home, since college had finished. I had applied for a job with United Airlines in East Point Business Park, in Clontarf. I was thrilled when my application was successful. I was due to start at the end of July but the date was later put back until the end of December. Though I had to wait a while, I was really looking forward to starting work. Mary had also got a job with the airline. The two of us would start on the same date. It would be a new beginning for both of us. I was grateful that Mary would be working with me. She had been a tremendous support to me.

After the atrocity of September 11 2001 there was great unrest with the airlines. Some of them went out of business and many were on shaky ground. Mary and I were left unsure of our new jobs. We waited for word from United Airlines and hoped that the news would be good. The second aircraft to strike the Twin Towers in New York was a United Airlines plane. I had to hold onto my dream. The job with United Airlines would give me the financial security I needed to leave Brian.

Brian controlled everything about our relationship, including our money. In the beginning I was working and that meant that I had a degree of independence, but that changed once I got sick. After my long spell in hospital I was on disability benefit. The disability payments were nothing in comparison to what I had earned when I was working.

This change in my finances brought about a shift in our relationship. Brian took on the role of breadwinner. My disability benefit was used for grocery shopping. Brian's money went towards utility bills and the mortgage. This meant that there was no paper trail to show that I had contributed to the household. This seems to be common in abusive relationships – the abuser controls the money. It is another way to exercise control over someone. It makes it very hard to prove that the person who is not in charge of the finances is actually making any contribution. I wish I had known this at the time, but I was too caught up in just trying to survive the situation and to build up my strength to escape. If I had realised that there was no paper trail or way to prove that I was living in the cottage, I would have ensured that my name was on at least one of the household bills. Brian had been clever in keeping my name off everything – even the deeds of our home. He had been generous in the very beginning and I suppose that drew me in. I hate meanness. As time went on and Brian became more controlling, he stopped being generous with money. I never knew when he would give me money.

Peter Joyce was still showing up at the house an odd time, although he was not as involved with Brian as he used to be. I think that Peter was easily led. He was a very quiet type of guy and wasn't pushy or intimidating. On one occasion Peter told us that his sister Amanda was in some trouble in England and that his dad had gone over to see her and bring her home to Ireland. It later emerged that her husband in England had been murdered and that he had been a well-known drug dealer there. Amanda had been questioned by the police. She returned to Ireland and lived with her dad and his partner in Finglas. Brian was spending a lot of time in the Joyce's home. I suspected that he was carrying on with Amanda but I couldn't prove it, and I didn't want to. She could have him as far as I was concerned.

ꕥ

I drove Robyn to school one day and headed back to the house. The driveway was filled with cars. It was so packed it was difficult to get the car in. As I tried to park, my wing mirror rubbed against Brian's car, leaving a scratch about the size of a hairpin. I went into the house and told Brian. He was having a bath. When I told him he went berserk, and with one punch he put his fist through the bathtub. I said nothing and walked away, leaving Brian in the bathroom swearing at me and calling me names until he was distracted by a phone call. He got out of the bath, dressed and left the house. Thank God.

There were many times that Brian lost his reason over small things. His temper was getting out of control and he became harder work as time went on. I had arrived home with Robyn and Conor from shopping one day and came in as usual by the back door. It was dark and hard to see until the sensor light came on as we walked up the drive. Nothing seemed unusual as we hurried to get in out of the cold. It was only when I opened the patio door that I could see that everything from the letter shelf was strewn all around the kitchen. I told the kids to wait outside the house and I went in to investigate.

It was obvious that the house had been burgled. I was nervous that there might still be an intruder in the house. I turned on every light as I passed through the rooms. It was clear that there was no one in the house, so I gestured to the kids to come in. I rang Brian and told him. Then I asked if I should ring the gardaí. He told me not to and then said he he would be home very shortly. I didn't clear up the mess until he had seen it. As I passed from room to room, I tried to put together a list of what was actually missing. There wasn't an awful lot of damage, but there was one thing that was puzzling me – there was no sign of forced entry. How had they got into the house when it was all locked up? No window was broken and no door had been forced. I noticed that all the locks looked fine and hadn't been damaged.

Something else had me puzzled. As I looked through the list of things that were missing, it appeared everything belonged to me. Some of my jewellery was missing as well as my music system, and so on.

When Brian came home, he walked through the house without saying a word. I on the other hand, was ranting about what I noticed was missing. Then I pointed out that it was only my belongings that had been taken. Brian went into manic mode. He got so annoyed that he picked up one of the pine dining chairs and smashed it to bits on the tiled floor. I said nothing, as I was in shock. After that, he left. The rest of that evening was spent tidying up the house. Robyn helped me. Even she suspected that Brian had staged it. I did too, but for what reason I did not know – especially as we didn't call the gardaí. Had he thought about claiming insurance and then changed his mind? God only knows what reason he had for staging a break in. It annoyed me that it was my stuff that was taken and I suspected that my belongings were given to Amanda Joyce as gifts.

The rows continued. Brian came home furious one evening, and I guessed that one of his business arrangements had fallen through. I knew that even though it had nothing to do with me, in Brian's mind it would still be my fault. I would be the one that would pay the price. We were snapping at each other. I was not backing down any more. I was sick of him. He went to the shed and came back with a petrol can and poured the contents all over the kitchen worktops, the cooker and then covered the floor. The smell was so strong that there was no doubt in my mind that it was indeed petrol. He then stood outside the back door and bent down to the floor holding a lighter in his hand, threatening to ignite it. I don't know how, but I knew he wouldn't do it. There was a flicker of realisation in his eyes and he came back into the house and proceeded to wash and clean it up. This was just another random act that proved to me that he really was going off the rails. I think one of the reasons that he stopped was he knew burning down the house would affect him. It was his home and he didn't want to lose it – I don't think he would have cared if I was burned alive.

Christmas was nearly upon us again. I had been shopping for presents and had decorated the house for the kids. I was determined that this would be the last year that the kids and I would celebrate Christmas in Mitchelstown Cottage. I was so worn out with all of this madness. I was tired of living in fear, and I wasn't prepared to allow another year of this hell creep by. I was about to make my escape. I was desperate for my children's safety. If I stayed with Brian there was no doubt now that he would eventually kill me. But if I left him there was the still possibility that he would follow me. I decided to take my chances and leave. I had to at least get my children out of there – out of that hell. They would be safe somewhere else, even if I was not. If it meant that my children were free, I would pay to see it through with my life.

Brian had started ringing cars: he would take the chassis numbers off crashed cars, put them onto stolen cars and sell them on to unsuspecting punters. There was always a selection of cars in the shed, and car parts were always strewn around the drive. Brian now seemed to have a new group of friends, none of whom I knew. They were always banging away at the cars in the shed, repairing whatever they were repairing. There was always a stench of petrol or diesel off Brian's clothes. I would often find car parts on the kitchen table when I got up in morning. This was another way of making a lot of money very quickly with a single sale.

I wondered how on earth he was getting away with so much. Word around the area was that he was suspected of being a registered garda informant and that may have been why he had escaped any incarceration. A few days before Christmas, Brian took the logbook belonging to my car (a black Fiat Punto). He drove the car to Drogheda and sold it. I went mad. I was due to start work at United Airlines and I would need the car to get there. East Point Business Park was a good distance from Finglas and there was no direct bus or rail service. How was I supposed to get from Finglas to Clontarf? I thought that he had sold it deliberately, to annoy me. I begged him to go and bring it back, but he refused. This was another attempt to take away my independence. I had a new job, but Brian was determined to get at me by stealing my car and making it impossible for me to get to work. It was infuriating.

It was Christmas Eve. I was in the kitchen when I saw Brian pull into the drive in a brand new metallic-green Ford Focus. When he came into the house he placed the keys in my hand and wished me a Happy Christmas. Then he pointed out the window at my Christmas present. I thought we couldn't afford a brand new car, but then the penny dropped. It was a ringer. I refused point blank to drive it, and refused to put my kids in it. He went mad and put his fist through the wall in the hallway. The car remained in the drive over the Christmas period.

I knew too well what Brian's game was. The car wasn't bought as a Christmas present for me. He was going to have it registered in my name, and would then sell it on at a later stage. If the car was discovered as a ringer, the responsibility would be mine. Brian was furious that I didn't fall for his trick, but I was still left without a car.

I enjoyed the remainder of Christmas Eve with the kids. We spent Christmas Day in Brian's parents' house in Drogheda. I had invited a couple who I knew quite well for dinner on St Stephen's Day. The couple were in a fix because their heating had broken down and they couldn't find anyone to repair it over Christmas. I was looking forward to entertaining them. It wasn't very often that I got the opportunity to have guests.

We had a lovely day. The dinner went well and we had a few drinks in the evening and shared a few laughs. I suggested that they stay over. They agreed and we made up makeshift beds for them. Their three kids and my two had a ball. They all slept on the floor in the living room, playing and making tents with the sheets. After breakfast the following morning, they left for home and I began to tidy the house. I was in good form and had enjoyed seeing the kids have such fun with their friends.

Then out of nowhere – and in front of the children – Brian brutally attacked me. I was subjected to the worst beating yet. I felt like I had spent several rounds in the ring with Mike Tyson. Robyn ran with her little brother into another room, both of them screaming. My body was completely covered in bruises from head to toe. He totally brutalised me. I was so badly beaten that I am sure that I was in need of hospital treatment. I couldn't move. I had to stay on the living room couch for two days because of my awful injuries. Robyn had to help get me to and from the bathroom.

Brian stayed away from the house after the attack. We had no visitors over those couple of days. I wished someone would call in and help us, or even come and see how bad I was. I was in such pain and still so shaken after the attack. I remembered Brian telling me that the two Finglas brothers were spending the Christmas holidays in Kilkenny, which meant that they would not be around either. On the third day, Brian tried hard to get me to go for a drive with him. He seemed rather anxious and tried his hardest to get me to leave the house. He tried so hard that it made me suspicious, and I became more determined not to give in. I figured out that he must have been expecting someone to call to the Cottage.

I discovered that Brian was expecting the Finglas brothers to drop in to the house. He was trying to get me to leave so that no one would see what he had done to me. He knew that the Finglas brothers would not condone his behaviour. I think he feared that they would retaliate in some way or shame him as a weak little man that got his kicks from savagely attacking a woman.

I stayed firm in my refusal to leave the house, and Brian eventually gave up and left. I waited for someone, anyone, to call and see my battered body. I wanted them to see what a small-minded sadistic piece of work Brian really was. I was just an object to him – something that he thought he owned and could kick around. I prayed that someone would see what was really going on at the cottage, what was really going on in our relationship and what must be going on in Brian's sick mind to inflict such brutality on the mother of his son.

During the years that Brian had been beating me, I had been very clever at covering up my bruises with accessories or make-up: sunglasses, concealer, foundation, scarves and baggy jumpers etc. I was so determined to cover up what was going on that I sometimes endured the jumpers and other heavy clothes during the hot summer months. I felt afraid back then that someone might notice the bruising. The thought embarrassed me. I didn't feel that way anymore. I realised that it was wrong to hide it away. I shouldn't be ashamed of was happening. It was Brian who should have felt shame. I realised I had had enough – I wanted someone to see what was going on. I wanted someone to see the hurt, humiliation and pain, to see my trauma. Having a witness would make it more real. Then I would know that it wasn't just the kids and me alone in this nightmare. I wanted Brian's sick and sordid behaviour to be exposed.

I saw a car come into the drive. I wasn't surprised to see that it was the youngest of the Finglas brothers. Normally, they would open the patio door at the back of the cottage and call Brian. This time I told him to come through the house. When he came into the living room he seemed shocked by what he saw: 'Holy fuck! Who done that to ya?' he asked in disbelief. I told him that it was Brian. He was shocked. He asked me if I was OK, and if there was anything he could do for me. There was nothing that anyone could do for me to make me right. I could only do that myself, but seeing the shock on his face somehow added to my confidence.

He didn't stay long. I think he felt slightly awkward and a little embarrassed. I don't know if the Finglas brothers ever discussed the beating with Brian, but I know that they were furious. Even if it was discussed, Brian would never have told me about it.

That was the last beating I was going to take from Brian Kenny. I was relieved that someone else had seen me that way – especially someone Brian was trying to impress. Despite the beating, I knew I was getting stronger. I knew my freedom was getting closer.

When the holidays were over and my bruises had faded, the children got back into their daily routines. Robyn settled back into school and Conor went back to pre-school. I took up my position as a Reservations Agent with United Airlines, and was enjoying it. I was studying hard too. A few weeks later Brian fell out with the Finglas brothers. He had not been spending much time at home, which was great. I could study in peace. I was still unhappy about driving the Ford Focus, but if it meant that I could get to work I would have to drive it. I had no alternative. It was important for me to get to work and to start earning my own money.

By early February the rows had again broken my temporary peace. Brian was making demands on me, this time involving his family. He told me to collect his grandmother twice a week and take her shopping. I refused. He came through the bathroom door and flung the car keys at me, hurting my hand as I tried to protect myself. The following morning, I went and visited my mam and I explained my situation to her. I told her how concerned I was about driving the Ford Focus. She agreed to go to the Finglas Motors dealership with me. She understood how important it was for me to buy a car of my own – a car that was safe and not a ringer. Mam went as a guarantor on a car loan for me. I filled out all the forms and my application was processed. I collected the car the next day.

I didn't say a word to Brian.

The following morning, Brian's dad arrived at the house. I asked him to drive me to my mam's house in the

Ford Focus. I then told him to leave it back at the cottage. He asked me how I was going to get home. I explained my plan to him. He was worried about Brian's reaction. At this point I really didn't care about Brian's reaction. I was ready for it.

That night would be the last night I would spend in Mitchelstown Cottage. It was 13 February 2002. I drove my new Ford Fiesta home and parked it in the drive next to the Ford Focus. I knew what I was up against and I knew that Brian would go mental when he got home, so I prepared myself.

We had not shared the same room in a long time and I was sleeping in the nursery. My plan was that I would go to bed that night with my red dressing gown on over my clothes. It had two pockets in the front of it. I placed my car keys, my mobile phone and some money in the pockets of the dressing gown. Brian had been missing all day and it was nearing 2.00 a.m. when I heard his car pull into the drive. I suspected that he had been out wining and dining Amanda Joyce, because the following day was Valentine's Day.

I could hear Brian open the back door, but I didn't hear him close it. I waited for him to come into the bed-room. My heart was racing. He came through the door, and, without saying a word, he grabbed me by the dressing gown and lifted me like a sack of potatoes. He carried me through the house and threw me out the back door onto the patio. He was shouting at me: 'That's insubordination, that's insubordination.' He locked the back door so I couldn't get back in, and turned off the kitchen light. He had done what I thought he would do. What he didn't realise was that I actually had my car keys and mobile phone in my pockets. I got into the car and drove quietly out of the drive, letting out a sigh of relief as I headed down the North Road towards my mam's house.

When I got to mam's the house was dark, so I called her on the phone to let her know that I was outside. She came and let me in. I told her that I could not take anymore from Brian and had left. She urged me not to go back but she was concerned about the kids as they were still in the house with him. She worried that he may be taking it out on them. I got back in the car and headed back up to the house. I was nervous as I approached – I prayed to God that the lights were out and the house was in darkness. If it was, I knew that he was asleep and that he was not tormenting the kids. It was thank God. So I headed back to mam's house, were I slept for a few hours.

At 8.00 a.m. the next morning I headed back to the

cottage to get the kids. I knew that Robyn would be up and getting ready for school and she would be wondering where I was. When I got to the house I could see Brian's dad, Billy, in the kitchen. Brian and the kids were there too. Robyn was dressed in her school uniform and Conor was still in his pyjamas. When Brian saw me, he unlocked the door and shoved Robyn out to me. I was not leaving until I had my son too. Conor was standing against the glass crying to get out to me and banging his little fists against the glass. My heart was pounding. I was praying that Billy would convince Brian to let my son come with me. I wasn't going anywhere without both of my kids. Then Brian opened the door, let Conor out and then locked the door again. I breathed an immense sigh of relief. We were out. We were free!

The following evening Brian's dad called to Mary's house. He was not calling to see if we were OK. He was calling on his son's behalf, demanding that Brian's house key be returned. I was shocked. I thought that it was interesting that now it was *Brian's* house – how quickly I had been cast aside. Mary could not understand why Billy was at her door making demands on me. She told me not to give him the keys, but I had a duplicate set, so I gave them to him. I had another set made months earlier after I had been locked out of the house. I swore that Brian would not get the better of me again, but I never got to use the extra set. I was so glad to have escaped with the kids that I didn't care if Brian wanted my keys or not. We had escaped from a nightmare. Our new lives together could begin. Just me and the kids – no Brian!

Chapter Seven

Life without Brian

After the kids and I left Brian we stayed with Mary at her home in Finglas. We slept in the box room, all three of us. It was small but comfortable and safe. It was a peaceful place compared to the war zone we'd escaped from. I knew that it would only be temporary because I had applied to Dublin City Council for a place of our own. It would take time to get a place but the wait would be worth it.

Brian was still harassing me with threatening phone calls, so I applied to the courts for a safety and protection order. I went to the Legal Aid Board and discussed my case with a female solicitor, Avril Sheridan. Avril was very supportive and gave me some great advice. She made me feel that everything would be OK.

In the weeks after we had left Mitchelstown Cottage, I learned that Amanda Joyce had moved into the house. *She didn't waste time*, I thought. I also discovered that Brian was dealing drugs again, and that he was enjoying his own product. There was no way on this earth that Brian was going to have custody of our son, especially now that he was dealing again and using. I would do my utmost to stop it. My baby son was growing up and achieving so much. I was sad to think that for someone so young, life had been so cruel. He had witnessed so much, and now his father would be absent from his life. The phone calls continued from both Brian and Amanda. I began to feel sorry for Amanda. She really did not know what she was getting into.

One morning Mary and I were getting ready to go to work. We planned to drop the kids off at school on the way. When we left the house, we were shocked to find that the passenger and driver's windows of the car had been smashed. There was no doubt in my mind that it was Brian's revenge.

I rang Brian, as I was fuming. He, of course, denied any involvement, but surprisingly offered to pay for the windows. He wanted to take the car away and have the windows replaced for me. I declined, as I was sure that it would be the last time that I'd see the car. I didn't own it outright and was still paying my car loan. I knew he could easily steal it – like he had my last car – and replace it with another ringer. I feared that he would put me into further debt. I booked the car into a glazier the following day, 13 March 2002, the same day as the court hearing for the safety order.

I knew Brian would be his usual cocky self in court that day. I just had to explain to the judge my concerns for my safety and that of my children. I had already been advised that five years was the maximum amount of time that a safety order could be granted for, but at the end of the five years I could reapply to the courts for an extention if need be. Brian joked: 'Give it to her for forty-five years!'

The judge granted me the full the five years, I was so relieved. Brian was instructed that he was bound to the court's ruling and was not to threaten or approach me in any way.

We left the court happy. Mary and I went to collect my car from the garage in Smithfield. We made our way along the quays. We had just arrived at the garage when we noticed a red sportscar approach us. The car resembled a Toyota Celica. At first I didn't notice that it was Brian in the car – I had never seen him in a car like that. Before he got a chance to get out of the car, Mary started to cause a commotion. She wanted to draw people's attention to us so that Brian would be less inclined to hassle us. Mary started shouting and waving her hands around in the air. She then beckoned and jestured for people to come and assist us. It was obvious to onlookers that something was going on. Brian made some comment out the window at us before leaving the area, aware that two mechanics had come to the front door to see what all the commotion was. Brian had received a safety order just twenty minutes earlier, and he was already coming after me to abuse me again.

Two days later, on 15 March, Brian broke the safety order again. I had driven to Finglas Village after working at United Airlines that morning. I was on my way to collect Conor from pre-school and had parked the car at the back of the building on Church Street in Finglas. I had just strapped Conor into the car seat and got into the driver's seat. I put the car into reverse, but, when I looked in the rearview mirror, I saw that a strange car was blocking me in. It was only when I looked in the wing mirror on the driver's side that I realised it was Brian. I quickly pushed the lock button on the doors. However, the window on the driver's side was down a few inches.

Brian was beside the car in no time. He pulled at the door handle and when he realised it was locked, tried grabbing at me through the window. He wrestled with me for the keys, which were in the ignition. Luckily he couldn't reach them. Conor was strapped into his car seat, crying hysterically. I told Brian that he was scaring the child and to go away and leave us alone. He was laughing. I couldn't move the car as he was blocking us in.

There is a taxi rank at the corner of the pre-school building and Brian was also blocking the taxi drivers who were trying to get up the hill. One taxi man interrupted Brian by rolling down his window and asking us if everything was OK. Brian apologised and said he would move his car.

As soon as I had a clear run, I sped off straight to Finglas garda station. Brian drove off. I reported the incident to the gardaí and I insisted that it was logged in the station's logbook. The garda promised me that he would caution Brian at the house in Kilshane. I don't know if he did or not. I hoped that he did, as I wanted to have some faith in the gardaí. I felt that I had not had their support in the past and I knew that I needed them to enforce the safety order.

I went back to Mary's house and waited for her to come home from work. When she got home I told her about the incident with Brian. She was fuming. I told her that I had reported it to the gardaí and made the young garda record it in the logbook. Mary wasn't happy with that; she thought Brian should have been arrested for breaking the court order and harassing me. She called Finglas garda station. A female garda answered the phone and Mary explained what had happened, insisting that Brian be picked up and arrested for breaking the law. However, the garda told Mary that there was little point in arresting Brian. She explained that he would simply be held in a cell overnight and then released the next day. This would antagonise him further and he would end up being even more hostile towards me. Mary was furious and hung up the phone.

Even though I felt relief at leaving Brian and felt that I could breathe again, I was also feeling quite down. Brian's constant interference in my life was playing on my mind. I didn't know how much more of this harassment I could take. I wasn't eating or sleeping properly and I was also experiencing panic attacks. Each time I had one it would be just as bad as the one before. I always tried to calm myself down and breathe, but it never worked for me. My anxiety would get worse the more that I thought about it. I often found myself on all fours on the ground, crawling around the house in a state of utter fear. At times I thought that I was having a heart attack. I actually felt as if I was going to die. I remember Robyn used to get herself into an awful frenzy when she saw me having a panic attack. Sometimes even small things could act as a trigger, for instance, worrying over a bill or being late for an appointment. Something as small as that could trigger the underlying problem: fear. When I look back, it is clear to me that I was suffering from post-traumatic stress disorder. What I had gone through and escaped from was going to take a long time for me to come to terms with. Even though I no longer lived in Kilshane, I was still affected by all that had happened there.

I remember on one occasion Mary accompanied me on a visit to see a Free Legal Aid solicitor. I wanted to know what my rights were. I collected Mary from her house and we drove to the office. As I parked the car at the rear of the building, I could feel the panic rise up inside me. I pulled at my jacket and thumped my chest as I could feel my breath shorten. Mary had never seen me have an attack before. Thankfully, she took charge of the situation and she soon managed to calm me down. That attack had only lasted a couple of minutes but they could go on for a lot longer.

Another time, Mam collected me in a taxi and the driver actually thought that I was having a heart attack. He was so concerned about getting me to hospital fast that he sped along the bus lanes, dodged traffic and cut corners.

I visited my GP about the attacks. She was reluctant to give me anti-depressant tablets, but wrote a prescription, just in case. She gave me a short course of medication, as she didn't want to look on my condition as long-term. I ruled out the idea of counselling, as I prefer to deal with things in my own way. However, I obviously wasn't coping well. I took the anti-depressants for two days. I didn't like the way they made me feel. I felt that I was reacting slower to people and events. It seemed as if I had no control. I decided to stop taking them and went back to my GP. She prescribed a week's supply of sleeping tablets. They helped me to relax but left me with a groggy feeling and a bitter taste in my mouth. I didn't ask for a repeat prescription.

Another month or so passed and I was back in the courts with Brian. Brian had applied for access to Conor and I was trying my best not to let him near my son. My sister accompanied me that day. Brian was accompanied by Amanda Joyce. That was an interesting morning, as the two shot smarmy looks at us. Mary wasn't at all unnerved by either of them. I just wanted to get it over with, because every time that I was in the presence of Brian all the horrible memories that I had came flooding back. We were sitting in close proximity to one another. I laughed from time to time as I watched Amanda Joyce looking through a bridalwear magazine. She deliberately positioned it so that I could see. I don't know what rubbish Brian was feeding her, but I had bought the T-shirt and worn it. There was no way I would be running out to buy a wedding dress. She would soon discover the true Brian.

We had the same judge again that day; I was delighted. Brian had already received the maximum safety order the last time. I hoped the court would come down on my side again this time. We were called into the courtroom and Mary and Amanda had to remain outside. I knew that Brian would want Conor to spend some weekends with him at the cottage in Kilshane. I prayed to God that he wouldn't be given access to Conor. After all Brian had already broken the safety order just two days later, on 15 March. I was concerned for the safety of my child, and I believed Brian was dealing drugs and that he was taking them. I was really concerned about Conor's welfare, especially if Brian was allowed to have him at weekends.

Brian was granted temporary access, which would be for four hours on a Saturday afternoon. I had to nominate someone to supervise the access for those four hours. The only person available to me was my mam, but I had to agree that she would supervise the visitation without her prior agreement. The rest of the family were taken up with work commitments. That was the ruling that day: Brian got four hours at the weekend and it was to be supervised by my mam.

When I got home to Mam's house and explained the situation she kindly agreed, and I volunteered Robyn to accompany her. I would feel better if my mother was not alone with him. Robyn agreed to accompany Mam as she also distrusted Brian. She knew what he was capable of. Robyn told me that she was concerned about her elderly grandmother being there with Brian for that amount of time each week. She felt that my mam would be quite vulnerable if she were left alone with him.

The first few weeks went well, though on a number of occasions Brian did not show up. I would drop them to Omni Park in Santry to meet Brian. I often got phone calls from them asking me to collect them as he hadn't showed. I kept a diary of every no-show. Brian did as he had always done: he pleased himself. It was clear to me that he was not bothered about Conor. He just liked to cause trouble for us. It was another way for him to feel that he had power over us and that he had got his own way.

My mam was great to agree to supervise the visitations. Unfortunately, Brian soon started to threaten her. He'd tell her that 'things could happen to you when you are out with me'. Mam was not afraid of him. But I was – so much so that I purchased a Dictaphone. I got Robyn to carry it in her bag. After the visitations I would replay the recordings. They were sometimes very muffled, drowned out by the shopping centre's background music. I hated the thought of the visitations and hated the thought of my kids and my mother having to meet Brian. The recordings were the only way I felt that I could make sure that my family was OK.

The court visits continued over the next few months. Brian had told me that he would be applying for full custody of Conor. He did this because he thought Conor would be financially better off with him than with me, he said. I was terrified of losing my son. I prayed that the courts would listen to me. I feared that if I did not fight hard enough for Conor that there was a possibility that Brian would win and have control of our son.

Brian's mam, Ann, also attended the court hearings. I didn't mind Ann having access to Conor, but I feared that she would allow Brian to have more freedom with him. I worried about what Conor would witness while he was with his father. The judge understood my concerns and it was agreed that my mam and Brian's mam would share the supervised access on alternating weekends at the shopping centre. This worked for a while, until Conor came home one Saturday with his hair shaved tight. I was furious. Conor told me that his grandmother hadn't been there. It was Brian and his sister who had brought him to the barbers.

I was in my mam's house when Conor came home. Brian, his sister and her two children brought him to the door. I was furious when I saw him. I had always kept Conor's hair long, as he had very blond eyebrows. I had planned on cutting it shorter when he got older and as his hair darkened. I gave out, and they left. I remember Brian insulting me by suggesting that I give Conor a bath, as there was a smell off him. Poor Conor overheared his hurtful remark. That made me very angry. Conor was scrubbed clean and he was wearing new clothes that day when he went out with his dad. Brian really tried his best to belittle us whenever possible.

A while later Brian's sister and Ann returned to my mam's house. Ann was giving out and had her foot in the door, making it harder for us to close it on her. His sister had told her mam that her kids were traumatised and hysterical after I had given out. I knew that this was nonsense and my mam agreed that it was an exaggeration.

Ann was panicking because she realised that she was the one that was supposed to be supervising that day and she hadn't been there. Instead of going with Brian, she had let him take control. I knew that having Conor's hair shaved was Brian's way of making the point that he was in control. My mam stood at the door with me. She told them to leave and pointed out to Ann: 'Brian's your son, Ann, and you will believe anything he tells you!' My mam was seventy-five years old and she didn't need this hassle. She was trying to protect us. As they left they called me a scumbag and an unfit mother.

I rang my solicitor, Avril Sheridan, and she told me that they had no right to cut Conor's hair. Avril said that she would send a letter to that effect to Brian. She told me that I was Conor's sole guardian and that no one else could make that decision, certainly not the Kenny clan. They always stood up for Brian and they always would. I was sick of the courts and I was sick of the Kennys.

Brian had no problem arriving at Mary's house unannounced while we were living there. This was a real shock, especially as Mary's home felt like a safe plave. She was so kind to us and really looked after us. One day I saw him walk up the driveway carrying something that looked quite heavy. I went to open the front door and Conor followed me. I didn't know Conor was behind me. As I was about to open the door to vent my frustration at Brian for brazenly appearing on Mary's doorstep, Conor reached for the handle and beat me to it. Brian bent down to Conor and patted him on the head. He awkwardly placed the object that he was carrying down in the porch. I knew immediately that it was some type of animal in a cage. Conor got down on his knees and had a closer look. He was delighted. Brian just smirked at me and left. I knew that Conor was happy with his new furry friend, but I was not. Again this was another way for Brian to get at me and for him to try and win his son's affection. Conor was really pleased with his pet. It was a black rabbit that he called Homer. What made him think he could decide when Conor got a pet, especially when we didn't have our own home?

I didn't know if Brian was deliberately trying to annoy me or if he wanted to please Conor – probably both. The arrival of Conor's new pet clearly put me in an awkward position. It was Mary's home and she was good enough to be putting up the three of us. Now I was going to have to explain the arrival of a rabbit. I am not great with pets, especially ones that arrive uninvited! I had enough to deal with without caring for an animal too. Conor was too young to look after it. Did Brian really think that a pet rabbit would ease Conor's pain or make up for the hurt that he had caused him?

Mary didn't complain as she was glad that Conor was happy for a while, and it seemed to distract him. I know that Homer the rabbit kept him company for a while, until he grew fed up with it. The rabbit was later adopted by a relative who lived in Sligo, and he promised Conor that he would look after him. I was glad that he had found a new home. The stench from the hutch when I cleaned it every day was enough to make me sick.

❧ ❧

It was the start of summer and we were still living with Mary, waiting to hear from the City Council about our new home. I was working away at United and I was enjoying my newfound freedom to an extent. I travelled to New York with my sister and we had a terrific time. We had unlimited free travel with United Airlines and we received first-class treatment on the way over. We were like two pampered pooches. We sipped expensive champagne and had a fancy three-course meal.

When we got to New York we visited all the sites and shopped in all the shops we had wanted to visit. We took the ferry over to Ellis Island and visited the statue of Liberty, which was a very significant moment for me as the monument stands for freedom. We decided that we would go and see Ground Zero. I remember the stench that hung in the air as we got closer to the site. I was saddened by the displays of photos and belongings of those who had perished on September 11 2001. There was a wooden boundary that stood as a perimeter around Ground Zero. It had photographs of all who were missing or dead. We saw photos of the flight crew that were on the United Airlines flight that day. We both cried – it was so emotional.

There was a platform that overlooked the site, and when we climbed it we could see the whole area. It was amazing. There were diggers and cranes clearing the debris. There was a large United Airlines flag on the platform for people to sign. We signed it as two United Airlines staff from little old Ireland.

It was my first visit to New York and it had been an

emotional and unforgettable one. I had never thought that I would ever get there. Life had been so difficult that I thought that all I had to look forward to was the constant fear of Brian Kenny. My life was changing for the better.

ᘓ ᘐ

On the 23 June 2003 Mary woke me during the night. She was whispering and beckoning me to come out of the bedroom and to be quiet and not wake the kids up. I got up and met her on the landing. She told me that she had just received a call from Brian. It must have been about one or two into the morning. She said he was screaming down the phone in pain, claiming that he had just been shot. She said she believed him. He told her to get me to ring his parents. I thought it was strange. Why would he ring Mary? She asked me what do. I told her to do nothing, leave him. I didn't care if it was true, as a part of me would have felt some relief if he died. But my conscience got the better of me and we decided to call an ambulance and the gardaí. We tried Brian's parents' house phone but we got their answering machine.

The following morning we listened to the radio news

to find out if there were any reports of a shooting. I wondered if Brian was dead. I drove from Mary's to mam's house to tell her the news. I took Conor with me, as Mary was heading to work and there was no one that could mind him. I was on my way along McKee Avenue in Finglas when I heard a garda siren. I looked in the rear-view mirror and realised that the car was chasing me, so I pulled into the kerb. I was a nervous wreck. I feared that they were going to take me into the station for questioning in relation to Brian's shooting. A garda got out of the car and I waited nervously as he approached mine. He went to the back door on the passenger's side and opened it. He then leaned in and told me that door was not closed properly. He then gave me the biggest smile and left. I was so relieved.

Amanda Joyce rang me later to tell me about Brian's injuries. Why did she think I cared? I had been hoping that he was dead. He had received gunshot wounds to his back and one of his legs, and I believe that another bullet grazed his head. Two armed men had come in through the front window of the cottage. Brian tried to escape through the back door but they caught up with him in the back garden and he was taken down with three shots. I know this sounds callous, but I was glad he felt the fear and pain that he had put me through. Brian blamed the Finglas brothers for the attack. It reminded me of the time one of the brothers had found me in a horrendous state recovering from Brian's vicious attack on me.

I had a couple of months of peace from Brian; I guessed that he was busy attending hospitals for treatments. But I knew that I would hear from him again soon.

ꟸ ꟸ

I was still waiting to be housed by the council and I was getting desperate. Although Mary never made us feel anything but welcome, the room seemed to be closing in on me. The kids had the beds and I was sleeping on a mattress on the floor. I still had pain from the surgeries and the sleeping situation wasn't helping. The kids were doing remarkably well, although Conor was not settling down at nightime. I had always stuck to a routine with the kids at bedtime. They went to bed each night at the same time. Robyn was seven years older that Conor, so she was allowed to stay up longer than her brother. Conor was not sleeping properly. I was worried about him. I would often have to call Robyn in from the street as she played with her pals, because Conor would not sleep without her lying beside him. I wondered what was playing on his mind. I thought that he was maybe missing Brian and the cottage in some way. He must have missed him and missed his home. It had been a big change for the three of us. Brian had stripped us of everything and left us homeless, and we were relying on the generousity of others.

Mary and I went to see a local Sinn Féin councillor and explained my situation to him. He knew of Brian Kenny and was aware of everything that I had gone through. He said that he would try to help. The council contacted me a couple of weeks later and told me that they had a house for me. They couldn't give me a date, but I didn't care – I was delighted and overwhelmed, so much so that I cried.

On 1 September that year Conor started school. I cried when I left the little guy into school. I think every mother there that day was crying. The assembly area in the playground was a sea of colour, with hundreds of bright-blue uniforms and colourful schoolbags. Some of the kids were excited and happy, although there were a few kids that were nervous and crying.

I collected my mam later that day and we headed back to the school to collect him. I didn't know that Brian and Amanda Joyce were sitting in their car outside the school, waiting for Conor to come out. When I came through the gates of the school with Conor, Brian approached us. I told Conor to keep walking and to ignore him, and I brushed past Brian. I got Conor into the car as quickly as I could. My mam was sitting in the front of the car. She had the door open and was insisting that Brian leave. He was hurling abuse at me. Then Amanda Joyce approached the car. I told Mam to call the gardaí, which she did. It was Conor's first day at school and it was being overshadowed by them. They went back to their car and sat inside it with the windows rolled down. I was so angry. I walked over to the car, leaned in the window and leered at both of them.

'See you, I'm not afraid of you,' I said firmly to Brian. Then to Amanda I said, 'And as for you, I'm certainly not afraid of you!'

They seemed shocked.

'You will be when you're set on fire in your sleep,' Brian said, stuttering.

'Very fond of fire, Brian, aren't you?' I shot back.

'What do you mean?' he asked.

'What about the garage you torched in Clonsilla, Brian? Will I tell the gardaí about that when they arrive?' I said. 'Oh, and by the way, Amanda,' I added, 'did he tell you that he torched your brother's car?'

She was speechless. She looked at Brian in disbelief. He didn't say another word. I could hear the siren of a garda car approaching. Brian started up the engine.

'Are you not going to wait for them, Brian? They're on the way.' I said sarcastically.

He drove away.

I knew that Brian was fond of setting fire to things. I wonder what Amanda thought. Joey had been left in Brian's car while he torched the garage in Clonsilla. Brian went back the next day to claim compensation for another of his cars, which was inside when the place went up in flames. He really had some nerve.

After the attempt on Brian's life, I refused to let him have any contact with Conor. It was too dangerous. Brian had to go to court and reapply for access. He was once again given four hours supervised access to Conor. Again this access was to be supervised by my mam. I was very worried about it. If there was another attempt on Brian's life, I hoped that it would happen when my family were not with him.

Again Brian would meet my mam in Omni Park shopping centre and spend some time with Conor. Once, when I picked them up, my mam and the kids were laughing. When I asked them what they were laughing at, Mam told me the funniest thing. She said that the centre had clowns and face-painters there that day. The clowns had been handing out sweets and balloons to the kids. She said that she had never seen anyone jump out of their skin like Brian did when the kids started bursting the balloons. She said that they sounded like gunfire and that he was petrified. She laughed and said that she would pay money to see that again. We laughed all the way home.

❧ ❧

On 14 September 2002 the council finally gave us a house. I was over the moon and so were the kids, especially Robyn. I didn't have many things to bring with me when I moved into the house. Anything that I owned before had been put into the cottage in Kilshane, and I had left there with nothing. I had a few friends that were very good to me. A neighbour of Mary's gave me a pine table with six chairs. It was in pristine condition and had beautiful blue tiles on the top. A friend of Mam's gave me an old sofa, which was great. I threw a bright bedspread over it that hid any wear and tear. It looked good. I was so grateful for these things. My friend Karen helped me to hang the curtains and do some of the painting. I bought a double bed for my room, which was delivered in a flat pack. Karen and I laughed when we took the parts out of the box. We didn't know which part was for what. Karen asked me if I was sure that it was in fact a bed. We sat on the floor and giggled as we tried to work out which part went where. We eventually solved the puzzle and assembled it. We joked about its possible collapse during the night and hoped that we had all the screws in place. Karen has been my friend since early childhood and we have been through a lot of ups and downs together. She is a rock.

The house was starting to take shape and everything looked clean and fresh. The kids had a bedroom each. My niece Hazel bought them both new curtains and bed linen that made the rooms look bright and cheerful. We were very happy. We had a home to call our own – just the three of us. Conor had settled in and was sleeping at night. Robyn was relieved that we were no longer under Brian's rule. We often spoke about the horrible things that he had done, and I tried to reassure her that it was all over.

I arranged appointments to see my children's school principals. I was worried that they, especially Conor, would be taken from school by Brian. Conor's principal took very seriously what I had to say. He made sure that everything was recorded in the school file and made Conor's teacher aware of the situation. He made me feel at ease. I am very grateful to him for his support and understanding during that time.

I then went to see Robyn's principal. We sat in the office for a long time chatting and I found her a great listener and a great support. She told me about the support that was available to me and said that she was also concerned for Robyn's well being. She offered counselling, which we accepted. She knew that I was struggling financially, and, every year before the start of the school term, she made sure that Robyn had everything that she needed. I am very grateful to her for her support and encouragement. She knew that Robyn was a bright child, and she feared that the past would hinder her studies. Robyn went to counselling a few times, until she felt that she no longer needed to. She completed her Leaving Certificate successfully, getting honours, and went on to college the following year to study social studies. It is great to find that there is support out there if you are strong enough to open up to people.

I had lived on my own before and it didn't bother me, but this time I was finding it hard to sleep at night. Since living with Brian I found that I had become hyper-vigilant of my surroundings. I had to investigate every noise that I heard at night. I would lock and double lock all the doors in the house and make sure that the windows were securely shut. I knew that Brian was getting into bigger things and I worried that he would actually have someone else harm me. I realised that not only had he battered my body and tortured my mind, he had also stripped away my trust in people.

One morning I received a social welfare letter. When I opened it I was horrified. Brian had warned me that he was going to apply for full custody of Conor, and now he had done it. The letter gave me the date and time of an appointment that had been made for a social welfare officer to visit my home and interview Conor. I was so stressed and worried. The appointment was for the following week, so I made sure that I had the day off work so that I could be there when the social welfare officer called to our house. I watched the lady as she made her way up the drive. I blessed myself before opening the door to greet her. She was very pleasant and did not make me feel uneasy. She explained that she was there purely to interview Conor and see how he was doing. I chatted to her for a few minutes, and, before leaving, the room I sat with Conor and told him to talk to the nice lady and not to be afraid as she was only there to see how he was. It was my choice to leave them alone, I could have participated in the interview but I thought that the social worker would see my presence as an attempt to influence Conor into giving the answers that she wanted to hear. I wanted her to hear how Conor was feeling, but most importantly I wanted her to understand that I had nothing to hide.

I sat in the bedroom and tried to eavesdrop on their

conversation. About an hour or so had passed when she called to say she was finished. I went downstairs to say goodbye to her and was relieved when she said that she had found Conor a very pleasant and happy child. She showed me some of the drawings that he had done for her.

As she was leaving, she told me that she would also be interviewing Conor again at his father's home the following week. She also said that she would be in touch at a later stage with her recommendation.

When she had left and Conor and I were alone, I couldn't help myself and I askedConor about the questions that she had asked him. He showed me the pictures that he had drawn. One of his drawings was of a house with Robyn, Conor and me, brightly coloured in. All of us were drawn with big smiles. He had circled a large bright sun in the corner of the page. He had also drawn a picture of his father – as Humpty Dumpty.

A couple of weeks later I received a phone call from the social worker. I swallowed the lump in my throat and waited to hear what she had to say. She said she was happy for Conor to remain with me and his sister. I let out a huge sigh of relief. I was so delighted and so, so relieved.

She told me that Conor was a very happy child and

loved living with his mammy. I thanked God.

Brian had stripped me of almost everything. If he had of been successful in getting custody of our son I think that would have been the straw that broke the camel's back.

I know that Brian did love Conor, but it was a selfish love. I feel Brian was incapable of a healthy relationship with anyone, even his own child. He would have smothered his son with everthing that he wanted, and in return Brian would have expected unquestioning respect and loyalty. I feel that as Conor got older Brian would not have had his best interests at heart. Without a doubt Brian would have led Conor down a road similar to his own. Conor would have been just another cog in the wheel of Brian's little criminal empire. I had seen what Brian had done to Joey.

ꕤ

It was Christmas week 2002 when I bumped into young Joey in Finglas Village. I was delighted to see him. Joey was in great form and told me that he was happy. I invited him to come to our new home over Christmas to celebrate with Robyn, Conor and me. I also had my aunt and uncle coming up from Wexford for the celebrations and I knew that Joey would enjoy it, as the entire family adored these two characters.

My aunt Nellie was an Elizabeth Taylor look-a-like and my uncle Jimmy was a gentle giant. Nellie ran rings around him. She was some character and everybody loved her, especially my mam. She adored her little sister. I think that every family has a character that stands out, one that everyone loves to be around. Nellie was flamboyant and glamorous. She had a knack of persuading you to part with your belongings, be it jewellery, clothes or make-up. She would arrive with one suitcase and go home with three. Through her 1960s Cleopatra-style make-up, she could turn on the puppy-dog eyes and you would give in to her because you loved her. Jimmy was the softest, gentlest man that I have ever met in my life. His love for his wife was unashamedly visible. Robyn and Conor enjoyed his company. He had a great way about him and children warmed to him quickly. I remember spending the summer holidays of my youth in New Ross in County Wexford, where my mam was born. Jimmy would bring Joe and me out to work with him as he delivered coal for Stafford's on the quays. We had such a great time. I learned how to play pool in New Ross. Joe and I would play at the back of the Regal Bar on the corner of Neville Street and Michael's Street. The owner, Denis Doyle, would allow us both in to play when the summer weather let us down.

It would be a memorable Christmas that year. Joey came and celebrated with us. The house was alive with laughter and music: guitars playing and everybody singing. We were all extremely happy. Joey left my house late that night and shared a taxi with my mam, making sure she got home safely.

On Christmas Eve that year Brian arrived to the house with boxes and boxes of toys for Conor. I was disgusted. They would dwarf what I had managed to buy for the kids that year from Santa. My presents would look pathetic next to Brian's extravagant gifts. However, to my surprise, Conor didn't open one of Brian's presents. I left them stacked in the hall and I waited to see if Conor would become curious enough to open one. He didn't. I was amazed. Even at the age of four it was as if he was making a protest of his own, or maybe it was his way of showing some solidarity with his mam. To this day they remain in the wardrobe, still wrapped in Christmas paper. I was very proud that Conor made that decision all on his own. It proved to me that he was wise beyond his years and that he knew his own mind.

Nellie and Jimmy went home to Wexford the day before New Year's Eve. I went for a drink on New Year's

Eve with Karen and her partner, Paul. We had a great night. On New Year's Day an old pal of mine dropped around and we spent the evening chatting. He was a lifelong friend and would drop in to check on us every now and then. When he had left, I opened a bottle of cheap sauvignon blanc, and sat and watched some of the music channels. I remember feeling so happy that I cried. I could not believe how much my life had changed. I was so proud to be moving on. I thought about how my children were coping amazingly well with their new surroundings and about how we had found peace in our new home. The kids had seen so much, especially Robyn, and they were adapting to and embracing their new life.

When I woke the following morning, I immediately reached for my mobile phone, which was on the bedside locker. I was feeling the effects of the bottle of wine that I had drunk the night before. I tried to focus on the screen so that I could check what time it was and saw that I had a number of missed calls. Three missed calls from my brother Joe and one from my uncle Jimmy. At first I thought that they were ringing me to wish me a happy New Year, but then I was gripped by the feeling that something was wrong. I immediately called Joe back and he broke the bad news to me. My aunt Nellie had passed away during the night. I couldn't believe it. I was in denial. I rang my uncle Jimmy; he was speechless and totally devastated. He confirmed my worst nightmare: Nellie had passed away quite quickly. I was brokenhearted and I was worried about Mam.

I had to break the news to the children. It was another difficult situation that they would have to face. They were brokenhearted and both of them sobbed. I visited Mam and she was completely devastated too. I offered to drive to New Ross so that she could see Jimmy, but Mam wasn't able for the journey, as she was still trying to deal with the shock. We all were.

The following morning, the whole family made travel arrangements and we all headed for Wexford. It was a sad journey. Mam and the kids came with me in my car. The journey seemed to take forever. I couldn't get there quick enough. I wanted so much to see my uncle Jimmy. I was worried about him.

I was driving through Graiguenamanagh in County Kilkenny when my phone rang. I handed it to Mam and she answered it. It was my cousin Breda. She broke more bad news for the family. Jimmy had been taken to Wexford Hospital, suffering from chest pain. Still driving the car, I sobbed uncontrollably. I knew what this news meant, and I could feel deep down that there wouldn't be a good outcome. I cried so much that I lost my focus and drove up a one-way street. I pulled into the kerb and tried to straighten myself out and console Mam and the kids. We carried on with the journey to Nellie and Jimmy's house to find the rest of the family waiting. We were only in the house a few minutes when the phone rang. It was the hospital. Jimmy had passed away.

I thought that God was playing a cruel joke on us. I was floored. How could this be happening? I was so devastated that my sister Mary wanted to get a doctor for me. I nearly collapsed a couple of times on the way from the funeral home to my aunt and uncle's house.

I thought back to the week that Nellie and Jimmy had spent at our house and I blamed myself. In my head I replayed everything that we had done together that week. Later I realised that nothing happened during the week to cause this. I knew that we all had a phenomenal time with them and my family were quick to point out that Nellie and Jimmy had a brilliant time in Dublin. I knew that. Nellie and Jimmy had a very simple and quiet life and everyone said that I had given them a great send off. It was their time to go and it was meant to be. Part of me was reassured that they went so close together. It made sense to me as they were such a close couple. They were buried together on the same day as my birthday, 5 January.

It took me a while to get over that shock. Mary and I stayed out of work for the remainder of January. We both had to attend the airline's doctor at the medical centre in Dublin airport. He agreed that it was a devastating blow for us. He informed United Airlines about our loss, and recommended that we were to remain absent until we were ready to return to work.

I feel sad writing about that episode in my life, more so than any other.

ꕥ ꕥ

In February 2003 Brian was still getting four hours supervised access to Conor. We were back in court and once again I had to argue my case and tell the judge about my concerns for Conor's safety. The judge that day said that she thought Brian should have more of a relationship with his son. She thought four hours a week was not enough and Brian agreed with her. I did not. The judge ruled that Brian should be allowed to have Conor stay over at the cottage every weekend. I was very upset and I felt let down by the system. There was nothing I could do. I would have to abide by the court's ruling. Brian now had more freedom with Conor. Conor stayed over at the cottage on a couple of occasions. I didn't know what he would encounter there. I knew what life was like in the cottage and I knew how crazy Brian could be. Conor was unhappy about going with Brian and the thought of Conor being out there without me made me very nervous.

On one occasion Brian came to collect Conor from my mam's house. Conor refused to go out to him and ran and hid under a dresser in the living room. Uninvited, Brian made his way into Mam's house, pushing past me, and grabbed Conor by the arm and dragged him from under the dresser. Conor was hysterical. Brian threw him over his shoulder and continued down the garden path. Mam and I followed him. She was shouting at him and pleading that he calm down and talk to Conor. Mam threw him a punch, God love her, as if that would persuade him to stop what it was he was doing. Brian ignored her and threw Conor onto the back seat – without a safety belt – and got into the car and drove away. Some of my mam's neighbours also witnessed Brian's crazy behaviour. We all watched helplessly as Brian drove away with Conor bouncing around in the back of the car, crying hysterically. The car door wasn't even closed properly. I was so worried for my child's well being. How could a court think this was actually good for my child? If the judge had only seen the way Brian treated his son, she might have ruled differently. If she only knew how Conor felt. Conor was becoming increasingly afraid and nervous of his father.

Brian was quick to make demands on me when it came to Conor. However, there was never any sign of maintenance from him. I never asked him for it, because I didn't want his dirty money. I wanted as little contact with him and his world as possible.

Another time, Brian was due to collect Conor from my house. I saw his car pull up outside, so I put Conor's coat on and told him to put his shoes on. I heard a bang on the door and went to answer it. I was disgusted to see that Joey was with Brian. I didn't even say hello to Joey. I am sure that he knew how disappointed I was with him. I felt betrayed. Joey had spent Christmas with my family. He had promised me that he would not go back to Brian. Seeing Joey in Brian's presence left me wondering if he had been reporting back to Brian. We had both celebrated our departures from the cottage together. I felt a great sadness seeing Joey fall back under Brian's control. I gave him a look of disgust. I think that he felt a little awkward when he realised how shocked I was. I was shocked because I knew what Brian's interest in Joey was, and it wasn't one of friendship or compassion. It was one of deceit, and one that fuelled a violent hunger.

I worried so much for Joey's safety. I hope that he knows how much I care about him, and that I still think of him all the time.

I met Brian's mam one day to drop off Conor. She was bringing him out to meet Brian as he was late and stuck in traffic. Ann told me that Brian and Amanda Joyce were to be married on 21 February 2003. She asked me if it would be possible for Conor to attend their wedding. This was Brian's request. I thought she was joking. I wasn't surprised that Brian was marrying Amanda: he liked to own objects and people. I knew that marrying her would make him feel more powerful and he would feel he had ownership of her. I felt sorry for Amanda. They had only been together about a year and she had not seen the real Brian yet. I too had received an engagement ring from Brian, on the 5 January 1998, my birthday. Brian had wanted to arrange the wedding for 1 July that year, his birthday. After the brutal attack when I came out of hospital, I had taken off the engagement ring and left it in my jewellery box.

I told Ann that I wouldn't allow Conor to attend the wedding. She tried to persuade me, but my mind was made up. I thought that she had some nerve, especially after everything she knew Brian had put me through.

ꙮ ꙮ

Brian had not only beaten and abused me, he had also robbed me of my home. An old friend had told me that the cottage was on the market and I knew that I had rights. I drove past to see if my friend was correct. I saw the for sale sign and took down the telephone number of the estate agent and called them to find out where they were. They were based in Dunshaughlin, which is quite a distance from Kilshane. Brian thought that he was being clever by not advertising the house with a local estate agent. He thought that the house would be sold before I realised and that it would then be too late for me to stop the sale.

I drove to Dunshaughlin with my mam and found the estate agent. I searched through the photos of houses and apartments that were displayed in the window. There was a picture of the cottage. I explained to the estate agent that I had an interest in the property. She seemed delighted at first; she probably thought it was a potential sale. Then I explained the situation to her. She was understanding and sympathetic. She took my details and promised that she would forward the information to me. She removed the picture from the display in the window. I headed home and waited for an angry call from Brian. It never came.

The next day I went to see a solicitor in Drumcondra

and explained my predicament to her. She wrote a letter to Brian informing him that she would be representing me. She contacted me about two weeks later to say Brian had not replied. She had tried several times to contact him but got no response. I considered the reprisals that were likely if I was successful in securing my share of the property in Kilshane, and I feared Brian's revenge. He was getting into bigger things and running an operation with a large and dangerous North Dublin drug gang. So I cut my losses and backed off. Soon after, Brian took the house off the market.

ꟸ ꟸ

In February 2003 I left United Airlines and went to work at Dublin Airport for an Israeli security company. I was responsible for the security of passengers and flights leaving and arriving on transatlantic routes. The new friends I made there were great fun. Though we had fun together, we also took our jobs seriously. We were trained to search both passengers and aircraft, using handwands, mirrors, body searches and personal profiling. We also had to carry out security checks on airport staff boarding aircraft. Homeland Security briefing letters from the US had to be signed by us, acknowledging any issues. I loved my job, but it was hard getting up at 3.00 a.m. to begin a shift at 5.00 a.m..

In April I applied to Servisair Globeground for a position as a passenger service agent. The hours would be easier for me and less exhausting. They contacted me to say my application had been successful. I was delighted to get the job and was due to start training in mid-June. I continued working in the security area until then.

On the afternoon of 17 April I was sitting with my colleagues Gina and Karl in the smoking area that used to be at Boarding Gate 23. We were waiting for the afternoon Aer Lingus transatlantic flights to depart. I had received a phone call from Brian earlier that day that had upset me. He was due to collect Conor from my house for his visitation time. As I was on a later shift that day, I had left the kids at my mam's house because I felt it was safer. Brian had been to my house and got no reply when he knocked. When he called, I told him that I had left Conor in Mam's and that he could pick him up from there. He was furious. I hung up the phone on him and continued working. Mam only lived five minutes away from me, so I didn't know why he was so angry. It would have been easy to call around to her house and pick up Conor.

I sat with Gina and Karl, watching the planes arrive and depart on the runway. We were basically killing time until our flights were due to leave. Suddenly, I felt unwell and I had three sharp pains in my chest and could not breathe. Gina and Karl were concerned but I told them that I was all right. They insisted on calling the Airport Ambulance. Then they both started giggling. I knew that they were bored and they just wanted to have a bit of fun; they thought that it would be very amusing to ring the ambulance. I pleaded with them not to call it, but before I knew it I heard the siren as the ambulance made its way up the runway. They thought that it was hilarious when the paramedics strapped me into the stretcher and whisked me away to Beaumont Hospital. I could have killed them both.

Karl got my car keys from the office and followed the ambulance to the hospital. I called Mam from the hospital, and told her were I was, just in case she was worried when I didn't arrive home on time. The doctors did all of the necessary checks, and a few hours later returned with their diagnosis. They were not sure what was wrong with me. They thought that I possibly had an infection in my trachea. I was given a prescription and sent home. I drove Karl home and then I made my way to my mam's house. When I got to Mam's, she told me that Brian hadn't come to collect Conor. I thought that was odd as I had told Brian that Conor was in Mam's. I went home and changed out of my uniform. I made some supper and unwound as I watched TV.

A few minutes after midnight my phone rang. I was just about to go to bed. I could see from the caller ID that it was Brian and I didn't want to talk to him. I didn't want him going off on one abusing me. It was late and he was the last person I wanted to talk to, so I let it ring out. It rang again another three times, until I gave in and answered it.

Brian's voice was calm and quiet – I was surprised. I listened to what he had to say. He was suspiciously apologetic. He said that he was sorry for everything that he had done to me. He spoke to me for about twenty minutes and told me that he couldn't collect Conor that day, as his dad had been taken very ill. He said that Billy had been taken into hospital and that he had gone with him. I told him that I'd also been taken to hospital, to Beaumont, because I had been sick at work. Brian asked if he could collect Conor the next day, Sunday, and I agreed. He ended the call by asking me to meet him for a drink sometime. I had no intention of doing that but I agreed so that the call would end. I was left puzzled. The week before he was furious with me, and then this week he was being apologetic. I could never tell which way he was going to be.

A week earlier Brian had arrived at my doorstep on

a motorbike on two occasions, dressed in black leathers. One of these times he had Amanda Joyce's child with him. He hurled abuse at me and threatened me. He was not due to collect Conor and I wouldn't allow him to take my son on the motorbike. I told him it was far too dangerous. Brian was furious when he left. Later that day, he came back again and threatened to shoot me on the doorstep. I took his threat with a pinch of salt.

When I got up the next morning I was feeling fine but I decided to take the day off work. I took the prescription from my dresser and went to the pharmacist to get my tablets. The doctor had prescribed two types of tablets; one was an antibiotic and the other was a painkiller. I already had the painkillers at home, so I just got the antibiotics. The pharmacist handed me back the prescription for the remaining tablets, should I need them at a later time. I slid the prescription into one of the pockets in my purse and went home.

Later that day Brian arrived to pick up Conor. I could not see any sign of a motorbike, so I let Conor go out to him. I hated letting Conor go with him; I was so worried about him. Brian stood at the door speaking to me, only this time he was calm and friendly. This cool, calm and collected behaviour made me wonder why he was suddenly being civil to me. I knew that Brian was up to something. I knew this was just an act; nothing had changed between us. I still hated him. There had to be a reason but I didn't know what it was.

ꕤ ꕤ

In May 2004 I was studying hard with Servisair. Even though I had been offered the job with with Servisair, I still had to sit an exam. The exams would take place in Clontarf Castle. I had to score no less than 86 per cent in each exam. It was tough going. I was having fun though and I was enjoying working there. I was also excited about my new position as a passenger service agent.

I was over the moon when I passed all of my exams. I felt that things were looking up for me. I had a lot of fun with the girls that I trained with, but none of them knew about the past that I had left behind. Working in the airline industry and dealing with Customs and border controls was not an ideal place to announce that you had been connected to a major drug dealer and criminal. That was something that I would have to keep to myself if I wanted to get on. It was hard trying to avoid certain conversations and lying when I had to. A lot of people that I have met in the past, either working with United Airlines, ICTS (International Corporation for Targeted Security),

Servisair or Aer Lingus@Stream would be shocked to know how much I hid from them. I had no choice. I had to protect myself and my job so that I could continue with some dignity and provide for my two wonderful children.

I still do not know how I have remained so strong. There were a couple of friends I made over the years who I was able to open up to about what had happened to me in the past. These were people that I had grown to trust and it felt right at the time to tell them. Although they could sympathise with me and understand to a certain extent, I could never tell them everything. I was afraid of saying too much and frightening them away. I was trying to rebuild my life, not knock it down again. I also didn't want to relive everything that had happened; some of it I simply wanted to forget about completely.

I could always have a laugh at work and I was able to forget about any worries. There is one funny moment that I will never forget. It happened at the safety training while we were doing our exams for Servisair in Clontarf Castle. Our supervisor, Kevin, had decided that we would share the class with some of the newly hired baggage handlers. All the girls were laughing and joking because we were going to have some male company. It was hysterical. Kevin arranged the desks so that they formed a square, and everybody took their seats while he remained in the centre so that he could demonstrate some safety techniques. Because we would be dealing with passengers and large amounts of luggage, he showed us the correct way of lifting a heavy item: back straight, knees bent, arms straight and lower yourself down to the item on the floor. Then we all had to demonstrate the correct way to lift an object from the floor and Kevin corrected us if we did it wrong.

There were about twelve of us in the room, eight women and four guys. Everyone else took their turn, and then it came to me. I jumped up and went to the centre of the square and proceeded to demonstrate the position. But just as I lowered myself towards the floor there was an unmerciful rip. The back of my trousers had burst open and everyone could see. I went into a state of hysteria and so did the rest of the class, although my friend Bernie was crying – I mean really crying: she was mortified for me. I, however, was completely entertained by the rip in my six-euro trousers from Penney's. I wore my jacket tied around my waist for the rest of the day. The guys got a great laugh out of that. The following morning I took my seat at my desk only to find that they had changed my nameplate. It now read: Rita 'The Ripper' Harling. I laughed and it stayed on my desk until the training was over and we were qualified. However, my laughing was about to be brought to a sudden halt.

ꟹ ꟹ

I had spent the morning with my colleagues at Clontarf Castle; we were wrapping up our studies and preparing to take up our new positions the following week. We were all in good spirits and were busy organising a night out together to celebrate. When all of our desks were cleared and we had said our goodbyes for the time being, I headed home to mam's house to collect the kids

I was driving home past DCU on Collins Avenue when my mobile phone rang, so I pulled to the kerb and answered it. It was a detective garda. He told me that he and a colleague were at my mam's house. My immediate reaction was one of panic. I asked him if my mam and the kids were OK. I knew it was something to do with Brian Kenny; it had to be. There was no other reason why the gardaí would want to speak to me. The thought went through my head that Brian had done something terrible to my mam or that he had abducted Conor. I was panicking. I asked him if it was about Brian Kenny, and he said yes. I told him that I didn't want to speak to them in front of my mam, as I didn't want her to worry. I also didn't want either Conor or Robyn overhearing what they had to say. I told them that I was on my way along Collins Avenue and I would meet them in Finglas garda station. He agreed to that and left Mam's house.

I met them in the garda station and was quickly brought into a small interview room where I sat facing them. I was nervous. They started the interview with a stern approach. They asked me where I was on 17 April. My mind was blank. I just could not remember. I had so much information stored in my head from all of my training and exams. They continued questioning me, so much so that my head felt that it was going to explode. We were nearly two hours into the interview when I pleaded with them to tell me why I was being held for so long. I had not committed any crime and I was feeling the pressure from the barrage of questions. They eventually told me that Brian was being questioned in relation to firearms. I told them that I had nothing to do with any of that and had no knowledge of any firearms. I no longer had any communication with Brian Kenny other than in relation to our son. It was very uncomfortable sitting there for so long. They offered me some coffee and let me out the side door so that I could have a cigarette. I was drained. I begged them to let me go home to the kids, but they continued with the questioning.

'Rita, you must know where you were on 17 April. Try to think back,' they insisted.

'I honestly can't remember. I know that 17 April is my niece's birthday, but I cannot recall where I was. Please let me go home and I will look at my work roster. My head is so full of exams that I can't think straight, and I'm tired.'

Three hours passed before they agreed to let me go. I left the station and headed to mam's to collect the kids. Mam was concerned but I told her not to worry.

When I got home I ran upstairs and searched for my work roster. I quickly scanned through the dates and times, and then the penny dropped: Beaumont Hospital. I ran down the stairs to the phone in the hall and called the gardaí.

'It's Rita. I remember where I was that day. I was taken to Beaumont Hospital from work with chest pain. I just remembered – I still have the prescription.'

'That's great. We may need to speak to you again tomorrow. We'll call,' the detective said, and thanked me.

'OK, but before you go, has this anything to do with the shooting at Cloverhill Prison?' I asked.

'Yeah,' he whispered, and hung up the phone.

Chapter Eight

The Truth

I was confused about Brian's participation in the shooting at Cloverhill. I didn't know what role he had played in the gunning down of Jonathan O'Reilly, who was shot by a gun man on a motorbike. I spent the remainder of the evening rummaging through presses in search of old newspapers, looking for an explanation, although there was no doubt in my mind that the gardaí had the right man. I could believe that Brian was the assassin. I remember seeing the RTÉ news report about the shooting and thought about the motorbike that Brian had arrived on when he threatened to kill me at my home. He was wearing a full black leather biking suit, and I was surprised by his sudden interest in motorcycles. But I didn't make the connection to the murder at the time.

I wondered why he had gone down the road that he

had chosen, but I knew that money, power and notoriety were important to him. He would do whatever it took to satisfied his craving for danger and excitement. He did not fear anything. He thought that he was untouchable. He was a compulsive liar but a lousy actor and it was hard for Brian to keep track of the yarns that he spun.

Brian was now involved with a violent Clondakin-based drugs gang. He was buying his supplies from them, mostly heroin and cocaine. As his dealing increased, he got more involved with criminal activity. However, there had been some feuding going on within the gang. The Doyle brothers, Paul and Simon, were the lead players in Clondalkin and the surrounding areas. On 22 December 2001 Simon Doyle was shot dead outside the family home in Clondalkin while his brother Paul was still serving time behind bars. The two had served time for attacks involving a cement block and a machete on two separate occasions. Simon was released a few months earlier than his brother Paul. I had never met either of these young men, and I wondered if these were the guys who had spent their weekends with Brian in the shed at the back of the cottage. I was still living in Kilshane when Simon Doyle was murdered on 22 December 2001. I had never heard Brian mention their names and do not recall him telling me about the slaying of one of these young men – mind you, we didn't speak much about anything back then.

When Paul Doyle was released from prison he vowed to get revenge for his brother's murder. The gardaí feared a gangland bloodbath between rival gangs trying to claim each others' territory. There is no honour amongst thieves, as they say, and there was a shift in the gangs make up. Les Rowan, Thomas Hinchon, Jonathan O'Reilly, Ritchie McCormack and Robbie O'Hanlon were all part of the Doyle gang. Brian Kenny was one of the Doyle gang's customers. However, the gang was having problems.

Les Rowan owed a lot of money to Paul Doyle. The amount was estimated to be approximately €44,000. Rowan had continued with the gang's drug dealing while the two brothers, Simon and Paul, were serving time. The amount that he owed the Doyles had grown. Rowan started looking for a way to get out of his debt. The gang wanted rid of Paul Doyle. They wanted to take control of their patch – the patch that they had secured while the Doyle brothers were serving time. The idea of wiping out Paul Doyle was appealing, especially to Rowan, as he would also be wiping out his debt.

An attempt was eventually made on Doyle's life, but he survived, receiving only minor injuries after he was shot by Rowan. Rowan went on the run at a later stage after he was convicted of additional drugs charges. Doyle managed to avoid being eliminated by the gang. However, he was convicted after a raid on his home – €340,000 worth of drugs was seized. It fitted right into the gang's plans for control of Clondalkin and the surrounding areas. The remainder of the gang began to feud amongst themselves: all battling for leadership.

Brian had been dealing with this gang for a long time and had become trusted. A close friendship was growing between Hinchon and Brian. Brian blamed the Finglas brothers for the attempt on his life, although he couldn't prove that they were responsible. Hinchon now thought that Jonathan O'Reilly was trying to take over from him and feared that O'Reilly planned to kill him. Hinchon felt that he would have to get to O'Reilly before O'Reilly got to him. Brian also sought revenge on the Finglas brothers. Brian and Hinchon came up with a plan. It was the perfect 'I'll scratch your back if you scratch mine' scenario. Brian would help Hinchon take out O'Reilly and Hinchon would help Brian take out the one of the Finglas brothers.

Unfortunately for young Joey O'Callaghan, he found himself slap bang in the middle of a murder plot. There's no way he could have even seen that coming. On 17 April

2002 Hinchon and Brian Kenny masterminded a plan to murder O'Reilly. Hinchon, Kenny and Robbie O'Hanlon concocted a plan to take O'Reilly on a day out. First shopping at Liffey Valley and later a trip to Cloverhill Prison, where Robbie O'Hanlon's brother was an inmate. O'Hanlon told O'Reilly that he needed to deliver some clothing to his brother. What O'Reilly did not know was that Kenny and Hinchon were waiting on the call from O'Hanlon. O'Hanlon left the car to go into Cloverhill Prison, conveniently parking on the opposite side of the road, leaving O'Reilly exposed as he sat in the front of the car on the passenger's side.

David Murray, a friend of O'Reilly's, had spent the day with O'Reilly and sat in the back of the car. Gordon Kelly, another known drug dealer, was also in the car. Kelly and Murray were unaware of what was about to happen.

Hinchon drove the bike that day, a Kawasaki 400cc, and Brian fired three shots through the window of the BMW, hitting Jonathan O'Reilly in the chest. After the shooting they sped off on the motorbike.

Brian Kenny shot Jonathan O'Reilly in cold blood. The thought of it made me sick. This was a person that I had once shared my life with. He was the father of my beautiful son. I often think about that day, and how I had suddenly felt sick in Dublin airport. Brian fired three shots that day at Jonathan O'Reilly, and I had three pains in my chest at around the same time that the shooting occurred.

I later learned that Joey had been forced to get rid of the clothing worn by Hinchon and Brian. Joey was told to burn the biker suits they had worn. I'm sure that Joey was terrified. Brian would have threatened him. I know Brian and I know that the only option open to Joey would have been to agree to his demands. Brian put the fear of God in Joey, as he did to me. He would have to do as Brian said or suffer the consequences.

Thankfully, Joey was brave enough to talk to the gardaí. I admire his mother, too, for taking steps to ensure that her son did the right thing. I believe Brian tried to reach Joey on his mobile phone to pressurise him into returning to the cottage. If Joey had gone back, Brian probably would have held him prisoner. Or maybe Brian had more sinister plans for Joey – he might have been trying to orchestrate Joey's disappearance, so he could hide his vicious crime.

ꙮ

One of the detectives who had interviewed me previously visited me at my house on a couple of occasions to question me further, as they wanted to build a solid case against Brian. Brian was trying to build an alibi by claiming that he had been with with Conor that day, which was untrue. I knew where I was that day and I knew exactly were my son was. Jonathan O'Reilly was someone else's son – I could not condone what Brian had done to him. It was soul destroying to think that someone could do such a thing and carry on, unremorseful.

The detectives didn't discuss the case with me; all I knew was that Brian had been involved. They questioned me about my life with Brian. I was as honest as I could be. I guess that they were trying to build a profile of Brian. They needed to know what made him tick and what made him such a complicated person. I could not give them all the answers. All that I could do was tell them about my experience.

As the weeks went on there were more reports in the media and things were becoming clearer to me. I learned that young Joey had been put in the witness protection programme as Brian and Thomas Hinchon had threatened to kill him. Joey had gone to Ballymun garda station with the support of his mam and reported the O'Reilly murder. In my eyes Joey was a brave young man and he did the right thing. I was worried for him though, and I knew that this would change his life forever.

I avoided going out or to shops for fear that Conor would see photographs of his father in the newspapers. Robyn was constantly worried that the gardaí would show up at the door. I felt sorry for the kids. I had to protect them. I felt sorry for Joey, too.

Brian Kenny and Thomas Hinchon were arrested on 12 May 2004. The rest of that year went peacefully for me. I was delighted that Brian had been incarcerated as I would no longer have to endure his abusive behaviour. However, I was still hiding myself away from reality. I continued working in the hope that no one made any connection between Brian Kenny and my family. I was beginning to enjoy my new freedom as it felt like the ties between Brian and me had been cut. I was enjoying my time in work with my workmates and the everyday banter that I shared with passengers as I checked them in at Dublin Airport.

It was the beginning of June 2005 when a young female garda knocked at the door. She handed me a piece of paper and apologised.

'I know you are probably expecting this and don't want it, but I'm sorry, Rita.' She seemed sincere, and she waited there until I had read the document.

It was a subpoena. I had been called to give evidence

against Brian in the trial of the murder of Jonathan O'Reilly. My nerves were shot. I would have to be brave.

Over the coming week, I told my family about the subpoena and they were all supportive. But they worried about possible reprisals, and so did I. I didn't know who Brian Kenny had been dealing with or running with. I was very nervous that week and couldn't sleep at night. I was now in a position that there was no getting away from. I would have to go to court and tell the truth.

I read all the newspaper articles that week and discovered the full extent of the cruelty that Brian had subjected Joey to. He had been imprisoned by Brian. I could sympathise with him; Brian had locked me inside the cottage many times. He made Joey stay within the walls of Mitchelstown Cottage. He was told when to eat and when to wash. Brian also subjected him to ferocious beatings, biting and punching him. Brian was worried that young Joey would tell the gardaí what he knew about the slaying of Jonathan O'Reilly. At one point he held a gun in Joey's mouth, threatening to kill him if he spoke a word about it to anyone. He also fired shots over the young lad's head when he brought him into a field at the rear of the cottage, putting the fear of God in him. Brian's behaviour had reached new extremes. He did everything in his power to ensure that Joey feared for his life. At that time he was a serious heroin addict, so he would have been paranoid and unpredictable. I prayed for Joey and I would support him by not giving Brian an alibi.

Thank God I got away from Kenny when I did. God only knows what he would have subjected my children to, especially when he was off his head on heroin. There is no doubt in my mind that if Joey had not reported Jonathan O'Reilly's murder to the gardaí, Brian would have continued with his manic lifestyle. If he compared himself to Tony Soprano before, I can only begin to imagine how large his ego had become by that time.

Brian had threatened to eliminate me before. I am sure had I not given him his way he would have had me removed in some way, either by having me shot or by staging my disappearance. So I have Joey to be grateful to for saving me from that fate. Joey's bravery probably saved a lot of other lives too, although he has paid a price. Living his life without the freedom to do the things that he wants to do without secrecy or fear must be very difficult. Joey is probably still reliving the nightmares of his abuse at the hands of Brian. I know it took me a long time to recover after I had escaped. Joey probably also suffered from post-traumatic stress disorder and might have also had panic attacks, like I did.

The week that the subpoena was served I had a visitor. I was expecting my friend Brendan, from Spain, to call to the house to see me. He rang me and told me that he was in Finglas Village and that he would drop in for a chat. I quickly tidied up and waited for him to call. I was lighting a scented candle with a match when there was a knock the door. I got a fright and dropped the match into the candle. I expected it to be Brendan. Still trying to retrieve the match, I opened the front door without looking out and told Brendan to come in. When I had retrieved the match and looked up I found a colleague of Brian's standing in my livingroom. I was surprised and a bit taken aback. He had obviously heard about the subpoena. I wondered what he wanted. Actually, I knew what he wanted.

He was pleasant enough and complimented me on my home. He told me that he had also been given a subpoena and that he was going to try to get out of it. I don't know how he planned to do that. He then told me that he had had a visitor to the cottage (he had been looking after the Cottage while Brian was being held in Cloverhill, awaiting trial). He told me that the caller told him to pass on a message to Brian that he was not to open his mouth, or else! He said the caller was a Kildare man and that he looked fairly affluent and didn't look to be part of a drugs ring. Brian's colleague told me that this guy had unnerved him about giving evidence in court.

I didn't know how to take this information. I wondered if he was trying to make me nervous about the same man showing up at my house. It would have taken more than that for me to change my mind. I wondered how could Brian's colleague still stand in Brian's defence. Why would he want to get Brian, a dangerous, violent and mentally ill man, off the hook? If he had been my friend, I would have disowned him.

Chapter Nine

The Trial

The trial was set for 16 June and was held in the Four Courts. The detective called me and said he and a colleague would collect me from my house early that morning. I tried to smarten myself up. My hands shook with nervousness as I applied my make-up. I sprayed Rescue Remedy on my tongue about forty times that morning. I wore a beige suit jacket, white blouse and black trousers. I made sure that I had a good supply of cigarettes in my shoulder bag.

I told Robyn not to leave the house. If there were any problems she was to call my neighbour, Sue, as she was keeping an ear out for them. I hated leaving them. I stood at the front door awaiting the detectives' arrival and dragged nervously on a cigarette. My stomach was doing summersaults. Eventually, the detectives pulled up right outside the house. I closed the door behind me, took a deep breath and climbed into the back seat. When we got to the Four Courts, I climbed out and lit another cigarette. The detectives made some idle chit-chat about my new job on the journey in. If only my colleagues at work knew how I was spending my day off. It was so surreal that I thought that I was dreaming. I felt like I was playing a part in a movie. I couldn't believe that I was there to give evidence in a murder trial.

We walked through the back gates of the Four Courts and I felt my heart race when I saw a number of people dressed in wigs and gowns. The detectives brought me into a hallway that leads to the Law Library. One of them opened a door and gestured for me to go inside. Above the door was a sign: 'Victims' Support'. When I went inside I was introduced to a lady. She was very nice and she sat with me until it was my turn to be called to the witness stand. She made me tea and tried to calm me. The detectives went back and forth, keeping themselves updated on any progress. I remember asking myself: 'How did I get to here?'

One of the detectives told me that the prisoners hadn't arrived yet and that he would accompany me outside if I needed to have a cigarette. I was standing outside in the courtyard, flanked by armed guards, when I noticed the prison transport vehicle arrive. Then I saw Brian Kenny and Thomas Hinchon being led along the hallway, both of them handcuffed. When I saw them I felt sick. The detectives crowded around me to keep me out of their view, but I caught a glimpse of them as they passed each window on their way along the corridor to the courtroom. I was ushered back inside and the detectives left the room to find out what was going on.

About an hour had passed when the detectives returned for me. I was brought into the circular hallway at the main entrance to the Four Courts building. It was filled with people. The prosecuting counsel came out to meet me and shook my hand and thanked me for coming. He explained to me what was going to happen and gave me some direction on how to present my answers, advising me not to elaborate or move off the topic. They wanted it kept simple, which made sense.

I was nervous and the detectives again brought me outside the main entrance for a cigarette. One of them stood on either side of me. Then I spotted Brian's dad, Billy, approaching me. One of the detectives warned him away quickly and Billy backed off.

I was then brought to the courtroom door and I could see people through the glass. I was told to look straight ahead and focus on the chair that was at the far end of the room. There were a couple of steps that I would have to climb first to sit in it. The detective told me that Brian and Thomas would be in the stands to my right as I walked along the aisle, and he advised me not to look at them.

I heard my name being called. The doors burst open and a number of uniformed gardaí came out to me. I knew what I had to do. I took the detective's advice and focused on the chair, and did not let my eyes wander in any direction other than that. I could feel Brian's eyes burrow into me, but I would not look his way. I mounted the steps and stood and faced the judge, who was seated at the same level as me. He smiled at me and thanked me for coming. The court clerk asked me to swear on the Bible, and I placed my hand on it. She smiled at me, realising my misunderstanding and said that I needed to take it in my hand. I smiled back when I realised my mistake. I felt stupid. I was sworn in and the prosecuting counsel started with his questions.

He asked me to verify who I was and if I had lived at Mitchelstown Cottage in Kilshane with the accused, Brian Kenny. Did Brian Kenny and I have a son? Did Brian Kenny and I part in February 2002?

'On the day of 17 April Brian Kenny was due to collect his son for visitation and never turned up, is that correct?' he asked

'Yes, that's correct,' I answered. If they did not hear me say 'yes', they would know what 'that's correct' meant.

The defence counsel did not want to question me. They were probably afraid to ask me questions because I could have given the jurors a clearer picture of Brian Kenny's character. The defence counsel would not want that.

'That's all, Ms Harling. You can go now,' were the last words that I heard in the courtroom that day as the judge dismissed me.

I climbed down the steps, still aware that Brian was watching me, still not making eye contact with him. I could feel his eyes follow me out the door. I smiled as I left the courtroom. I felt proud of myself. I had done what I had come to do. I felt stronger and I felt that I had stood up to Brian Kenny. I was no longer going to be intimidated by him. I think that he thought that there was no way I would give evidence against him. I'm not afraid of much any more. He has made me a stronger person. It's strange to think that, especially as it is probably the last thing Brian would have imagined when he abused me. His treatment of me has actually made me stronger.

I wondered how young Joey was doing. Was he waiting in the wings somewhere, nervously hoping that the jury would believe his story? I knew that I would not get to see him. He was probably waiting in a different part of the building. My heart was with him.

The detectives accompanied me home. They told me that they would let me know what the sentence was. When we got to my house, they got out of the car and shook my hand. They thanked me and told me that I was a very brave woman. Then they left. I no longer had anyone's protection. The job was done and now I would have to move on. I had played my part – an important part.

I replied to the the many missed calls from family members and friends. They were all curious and concerned about the outcome of the case, and they were all worried about my well being. Robyn followed me around the house for the rest of that day. I knew that she was concerned as well. That night I sat on the edge of the bed staring out the window waiting for something to happen. I did the same thing every night that week. I was nervous of the unknown. I was so unsure about the outcome of the trial. I prayed to God that justice would be done, and that Brian would receive the sentence he deserved.

One of the detectives sent me a text later that week telling me the outcome of the trial. On July 5 2005 Mr Justice Peart sentenced both Brian Kenny and Thomas Hinchon to life for the murder of Jonathan O'Reilly.

Brian was also handed down two additional three-year sentences for threatening Joey's life and for possession of firearms and ammunition. Thomas Hinchon received an additional eighteen months, also for threatening Joey's life. By my calculation, Brian would serve between eighteen and twenty-one years, although nobody has given me a definitive number. I am still unsure of his release date. Conor will be a grown man by then, and God knows where life will have brought us to by that time.

When Brian was arrested, he was held in Cloverhill Remand Prison in Clondakin. He remained there for some time after the trial. However, he has since been moved to Mountjoy Prison in Dublin 7, which is a higher-security facility. I believe that he now spends twenty-three hours a day in solitary confinement. I often wonder what goes through his mind now, especially as he has a lot of time to think. I sometimes wonder if he feels remorseful about what he did. Does he regret the past? Does he regret the hurt that he put other people through? Does he think about his family and what he put them through? Does he ever think about Jonathan O'Reilly's family? Does he realise that his actions, cruelty and extreme violence caused so much pain and suffering?

After Brian's arrest Amanda Joyce gave birth to Brian's

second son. Brian's behaviour over the years has now left two children without the love and support of their father. I regret that Conor will grow up not knowing his father. Brian will never kick football with him or teach him how to swim, fish or ride a bike, and Conor will grow up without those memories. That's a sad fact. Conor has never asked to visit his father in Mountjoy, which doesn't surprise me. Robyn and I would prefer to forget about Brian Kenny, so he won't be getting a visit from either of us. I'm not sure how much his own family visit him. I have no idea about the visiting rules in prison, and I don't want to either.

When I think back to the day that I accepted a lift from him, and remember how he laughed and joked with Robyn, it's hard to believe that he ended up in prison for murder. Not only have his actions ended a young man's life, but they have also made a total waste of his own.

Brian had choices and he chose a life of destruction. He had two chances of a family life. When we set up home together, we had all the regular things most couples aim for: we both had good jobs, we had a mortgage, but most of all we had two wonderful children to share our home. Brian destroyed all that. He got a second chance with Amanda Joyce and he destroyed it again. I wonder if he ponders his choices during his twenty-three hours in solitary confinement.

ꕥ ꕥ

The Clondalkin gang continued to reap the rewards of their cruel regime. Jonathan O'Reilly was dead as a result of their greed. His so-called friends, Brian Kenny and Thomas Hinchon, were serving life behind bars for his assassination. Robbie O'Hanlon continued to deal drugs until he was shot dead while taking part in a football match near Liffey Valley shopping centre. He was shot three times to the head and chest. I read an article about him and it seems that he was a nasty piece of work. He was a very violent man and on one occasion he was violent towards his girlfriend. I read how he had brutally beaten her with a sweeping brush-handle until it broke in the middle. Brian had done the same thing to me. Robbie's girlfriend had him charged and he spent some time in prison for the offence. I have to admire her courage. She was a brave girl indeed, and should be very proud of herself.

Another member of the Clondalkin-based gang was also murdered a year later. Ritchie McCormack was shot dead outside his brother's home. Paul Doyle was the only remaining member of this group. He was still in prison serving time for the drug raid that was carried out at his home in 2003. He received a five-year sentence with the last year suspended. The gang had broken up by the time Doyle was released from prison. I wonder if he learned anything from his time in prison and has moved on with his life. The gang may have broken up, but drugs will never disappear. They will always be a part of our world. There will be someone else to pick up where they left off.

ൈ ೋ

The days turned to weeks and the weeks to months, and I was feeling great to be free of Brian. I was enjoying planning for the future. After work one day, I dropped in on Mam to see how her day was going. She was well when I got to the house, but she seemed a little quiet. When I asked her what was wrong she dismissed it by saying: 'Nothing'. I wasn't happy with that, so I asked again. She told me that she had received a phone call earlier and that she was a bit confused about it. She explained that the call had come from Brian. I was in shock. How could this be? Surely they don't have this privilege in prison? She said that he wanted her to ask me to forward photographs of

Conor to him at Cloverhill.

I also knew that Mam was holding something back. She wasn't telling me everything. She seemed worried and I wondered if Brian had threatened her. I knew that Mam was a strong lady, but I also knew that Brian could prey on her vulnerability as an elderly person living alone. I begged her to tell me what else Brian had said, and she eventually gave in and told me.

She said that Brian had called from his cell, and that he had told her that he was sharing a cell with Liam, Jock Corbally's son. I think Mam was a bit gobsmacked by this, or maybe she was remembering her friend Maureen Corbally, who had died a few years earlier from cancer. Liam was Maureen's grandson. My Mam had befriended Maureen in the early eighties. The two women had met on a bus and they became close friends.

I remembered back to the time that Jock Corbally went missing, and recalled Mam telling me how upset and distraught Maureen was. I remember Mam's concern and I recall Maureen and her family's anguish. It was 1996, a year that was marked with blood. The murder of Jock Corbally on 28 February 1996 was reported in all the newspapers. I was living in the cottage in Kilshane with Brian at the time and working at the Esso garage at the top of the hill on the Old Finglas Road, about a hundred metres from The Royal Oak pub. It was a time when the criminal world was becoming more dangerous, as gangsters moved from thieving to dealing drugs and fighting over territories.

I heard that Jock had his teeth pulled out and that he was beaten and stabbed repeatedly and then buried alive in an unmarked grave. It was horrific. I remember Mam praying for Maureen. The Corbally family were traumatised by Jock's disappearance and murder. His body has never been found.

Finglas is not a huge place and the community is tight. I would say that every person living in Finglas knows of someone who either deals or takes drugs. The people of Finglas and the voluntary organisations that operate there have worked hard to try to wipe out this problem that has been tearing the community apart for so long. They have never given up and the battle continues.

Mam was clearly upset by Brian's phone call. She was very quiet, which was not like my mam. She seemed deep in thought when I asked her what she was thinking about, and she sounded troubled. Mam told him that there was no chance of me sending photos to him. That would have annoyed him. I stayed in the house with her for a while before heading home. Before I left I rang a detective and told him that Brian Kenny had a phone in his cell and that he was intimidating my mam. I wanted the prison governor alerted to the fact and I wanted the phone confiscated. Mam never heard any more from Brian.

❧ ☙

Sometimes I worry about Conor having been exposed to so much criminality. I can only hope that he does not go down that road. Drugs are now everywhere in our society. I have lived in Finglas most of my life and I have met wonderful people there; most of them are 'the salt of the earth'. Over the last number of decades Finglas has had a bad reputation. It is a working-class area with all of the usual problems that any local authority area has, with few recreational facilities for younger adults. Sometimes I find it painful to read about Finglas in the newspapers. I have nothing but good memories of the place. I had an excellent childhood and my parents were loving and wanted the best for us. Like my parents, there are many others in Finglas who love their children and want them to do well. But life doesn't always work out like that. You can never tell what the future will hold for any child. My mother did not raise me to become Brian Kenny's personal punch bag. It is a horrible feeling to have someone control you. You are left feeling alone and in despair. You cannot see your future. All that you can see ahead of you is continued abuse, until one morning you wake up and smell the coffee. Some are lucky; they wake up to the facts earlier than others. Unfortunately, some wake up too late and it's too late to do anything.

༄ ༄

My relationship with Brian Kenny was very different to my previous relationships. I have very fond memories of some of my old boyfriends. I got through my teens with ease and enjoyed my freedom and my friends. I dated a young man called Gerry Bennett from the age of sixteen until I was twenty-one. Gerry was also from Finglas and he came from a large respected family. We were very innocent back then. I bought Gerry his first guitar about two years into the relationship. Gerry's younger brother, Charlie, and their friend Jimmy Taigue formed a band called The Missing Link. They hooked up with another young man called Terry, who was also from Finglas. Terry was the drummer in the band. I enjoyed jamming with them in the shed at the back of the Bennetts' house. They were so dedicated and ambitious. Jimmy was the lead guitarist and he taught both Gerry and Charlie how to play the guitar, Gerry on rhythm and Charlie on bass. I got on really well with them. I was one of the lads. The band played together daily, and I would join in on some of the harmonies with Jimmy.

I have great memories of them all. The band worked hard and became quite popular in Finglas and played gigs at The Underground on Dame Street. One evening they backed up Paul Cleary and The Blades at the Olympia Theatre. I was so proud of them. I loved going to recording studios in Dublin and watching the guys record their demo tapes. They won the Battle of the Bands one year, beating A-House and Those Handsome Devils.

Jimmy was a genius; he could pick up any instrument and play it.

We would spend our summers in the Bennetts' mobile home in Loughshinny, close to Rush and Skerries in North Dublin. Jimmy was a real entertainer, a natural. I remember him allowing me to apply make-up to his face one day as we sat in the mobile home, the rain pouring down outside. I often smile when I think of him. We had great times back then, singing and playing guitars on the harbour.

They hired a new manager, Mick Neary. Mick was a great choice as he shared the same humour as the guys and they got on really well. Jimmy, Mick and I all worked at the same Esso garage and we shared some great times.

I think I laughed every day in those days. Life was sweet. The guys were always playing tricks on me. It was pure innocent fun. I think that I was a bit of a tomboy really. I had bought a Suzuki 'Love' moped because sometimes I would have to work the late shifts at the garage. As there was no bus service, it was a handy way for me to get home. I remember getting ready to go home one evening when Mick and Louis were on the roof cleaning the fascia boards above the garage. I said my goodbyes and went to get my moped, which was parked under the service hatch. I had just sat on the bike and put the key in the ignition when down came two buckets of dirty smelly water. I remember laughing so hard and I could hear the two culprits on the roof, in flitters. They thought that it was hysterical. I was soaked. I knew that the water was dirty because I could feel it's gravely texture in my hair, and I think I even swallowed some. I remember shouting at them and calling them names, and laughing as I did. They wouldn't come down from the roof. We continued to laugh uncontrollably and so did the couple of customers who were on the forecourt.

I loved the people that I worked with there. They were all great characters. Linda Porter was a great friend and we shared many laughs together. Michael Chawke, the manager, has to be the best boss that I have ever had. Carl, who worked the evening shifts, had the most infectious laugh. Liam, Sean and Donagh: they were all very different characters and great fun. I wonder what they are all up to nowadays. I know that Donagh Diamond is now working for RTÉ as a reporter. I was heading home one night and Donagh had just taken over from me. The wind was howling outside. I could see that the trees in the cemetery across the road were bending. The headlight on my bike wouldn't turn on. I was worried about getting home safely. Donagh had the bright idea of getting one of the huge box torches and taping it onto the bike. We fell around the place laughing as I ventured out into the crazy weather. I was in fact heading into Hurricane Charlie. I don't know how on earth I got home in one piece that night, as the wind and rain made it nearly impossible to see through the visor of my helmet. I was surprised that the bike didn't lift off the road as it was so lightweight – maybe it was the weight of Donagh's box torch that did the trick.

Gerry and I eventually broke up and we both moved on with our lives in different directions. The band continued to gig and jam together. They later secured a record deal with EMI/Sony Records, and were a successful rock band. In the meantime I had met Robyn's dad and settled with him for a few years.

ꙮ

In 1997, when I was pregnant with Conor, I learned of my dear friend Jimmy's death. Sadly Jimmy had battled with multiple sclerosis (MS) for some years, but lost his battle in the end. It was a waste of such a talented young man's life. Life seems to be incredibly unfair sometimes.

ꙮ

I don't think that I will ever fully get over the abuse that Brian put me through. However, I am learning to deal with the past as best I can, and, as time goes by, I am trying to forgive. It has not been easy. Abuse, no matter what form it takes, is horrific. Whether it is physical or psychological, it can leave a person scarred for life.

To any woman that is out there right now going through some form of abuse, I urge you to dig deep down into your soul, pull your strength from it and get out. You are worth more than that, and so are your children, if you are lucky enough to have any. Look to your family and friends for support. Don't be afraid to talk about it, and, ultimately, do not in any way feel ashamed. These men are brutes. They take some sick pleasure in abusing you. No one has a right to say a single evil nasty word or to lay a hand on you. I cannot understand why some men and women think that they have the right to carry out these acts on another person. Who or what gives them the right? I feel sorry for some of them, as they obviously have issues that they need to deal with themselves. This does not excuse them for taking out their troubles on others. Don't let them use the sympathy card to justifiy their actions. Brian was good at turning on the water works when he wanted to. I fell for it in the beginning, but thankfully I listened to my inner-self. I was crying too on the inside and nobody could tell, until I was brave enough to tell the people around me. I think that when you reach that point – the point when you no longer hide what is happening to you – then you are getting ready to leave.

I am dedicating this book to the memory of another mum of two, who found herself in a similar situation to mine – although the outcome for her was tragic. Baiba Saulite, a young Latvian woman, was gunned down outside her home in Swords, as she stood in her front garden with her friends. A lone gunman wearing a baseball cap walked briskly up to Baiba and pumped two shots into her chest, killing the innocent young mother. When I think that Brian threatened to have me eliminated, I often remember Baiba's killing and feel great sympathy for her. Money and power are these men's gods and they have no respect for human life. I hope that people do not forget this brave young mum who will never see her children grow up. No one has yet been arrested for the brutal slaying of Baiba Saulite.

༄ ༄

When things had settled down after the trial, I began to speak to my children about their thoughts and feelings. I realised that they too harboured great resentment towards Brian, especially Robyn. She cried when she remembered some of the brutal events that she had witnessed while we lived with him. She also cried when she spoke of our departure from Mitchelstown Cottage. I feel so remorseful that my children were subjected to such cruelty. I would never have dreamt of bringing them down that road had I known what a monster Kenny really was. Living with Brian has scarred all three of us.

Around this time Conor made his First Holy Communion. I was looking forward to the day and was happy that we were moving forward with our lives. Robyn and I were sitting in the church beside Conor, who looked dapper in his suit and tie. Robyn was fidgeting in her seat and watching all of the commotion that was going on around her as the teachers tried to get the young pupils into their allocated seats. Conor sat smiling at his classmates. Mass had just begun when I felt Robyn nudging me.

'Mam! Mam!' she whispered.

I looked at her, slightly annoyed that she was talking in church:

'What?' I asked.

'The Kennys are here,' she said, 'the lot of them.'

'Where are they?' I asked. I couldn't believe that they were in the church.

'About six rows behind us,'

'I don't believe this!' I muttered to myself, as I took a deep breath.

I had not seen or heard from the Kennys in over a year, since Brian's arrest. Now here was the whole clan behind me, on this of all days. It was supposed to be Conor's special day, not a reminder of what we had escaped from. I could feel their eyes were on us. I didn't know how to take their sudden arrival at first. I was shocked. They had not received an invite or contacted me about Conor at all, but here they all were making their presence felt. The mother, father, brother and both sisters had come. Someone had obviously gone out of their way to find out from either the church or the school the date and time of the First Holy Communion ceremony. My family were not present with me that day because we had arranged to visit them all later, after the ceremony. I now felt hugely intimidated by the Kennys' presence. They had some nerve. I couldn't enjoy the Mass. I told Robyn not to look behind at them, and we didn't tell Conor that they were there.

Instead of enjoying my son's First Holy Communion I wanted it to end. I had to walk Conor up to the altar to receive Communion, so I knew that all eyes would be on us as we made our way back to our seats. I kept my focus on the floor and didn't acknowledge the Kennys. As soon as the priest had given his final blessing and Mass had ended, I ushered the kids out of their seats quickly. We slipped out the side door and headed for the car as quickly as possible. Conor couldn't understand why he couldn't stay and talk to his friends. I was annoyed that I wouldn't get any photographs of Conor on the altar or with his teacher. The Kennys had cut Conor's day short. I don't know what Brian's family hoped to achieve that day. I'm glad that Conor didn't know they showed up. He had a good day, and that was all that mattered to me.

ꟷ

Conor told me things that had occurred while he spent time with his father. One horrific story stands out. Conor remembers sitting at the kitchen table in the cottage with Joey and another child. When Brian served dinner, the other child refused to eat it. Brian became very angry and started shouting and demanding that the child eat the food he had prepared for him. The boy still refused. When Brian saw that his methods were not working on the seven-year-old child, he did something disgusting that shocked both Conor and Joey. Brian went and got a tin of dog food, emptied it onto a plate and made the child eat it. Conor said that he felt sick and that he was very afraid. Conor didn't tell me at the time because he knew that I would go mad. He knew that I would have confronted Brian and a full-scale row would have erupted. Then Brian would have threatened me and might have even become violent. Even as young as Conor was, he had been clever enough not to tell me. He was trying to protect me.

Conor told me that on another occasion, Brian put him on the back of a motorbike and drove from Dublin to Drogheda. I was horrified. Conor told me that he was sweating because he was trying to hold on to his dad's slippery leather jacket. He found it hard to hold on because Brian was driving so fast. Conor was just seven at the time. Can you imagine how a seven-year-old would have felt trying to hold on for that long journey? If Conor had come off the back of that bike while it was travelling at speed, he would have been killed. I suspect the motorbike was the same one that was used in the shooting of Jonathan O'Reilly – the Kawasaki 400 cc. Brian obviously had no respect for life, not even for that of his own son. Conor was terrified of Brian. He put on a show for Brian: he was always smiling, but was really afraid to say or do the wrong thing in front of him.

Robyn spoke to me about the conversations she had with Joey. She told Joey how much she hated Brian. Unbeknownst to me, Brian had been abusing my daughter, not physically, but emotionally and mentally, by insulting her whenever he could, and always out of my earshot. This made me very sad. I knew that Brian was sly about what he was putting her through. If he started beating her, I would have known and done something about it. The fact that he was insulting her and saying cruel things to her out of my earshot, made it impossible for me to defend her. I didn't know at the time what he was doing. She never told me because she was afraid that things would escalate, and she didn't want to put me through that. She was so young and unaware that she was putting herself through her own battle.

Brian locked her out of the house on a few occasions

when I was not at home. She remembers sitting on the garden seat in the freezing cold as Brian and his companion sorted bars of hashish, microwaving them and cutting them into smaller pieces, paying no attention to her. She saw Brian wrap a gun up in a white plastic bag and hide it in a tree in the back garden. Not only did Brian have a gun in the house on more than one occasion, but my daughter had to see it. She must have been terrified. What would have happened if Conor had come across it when he was playing in the garden?

Robyn's bedroom was in the attic. It was a small room and could only accomodate someone her size and age in any comfort. She loved that little room. It was like her secret little cave. I had decorated it and painted the *Rug Rats* and *One Hundred and One Dalmatians* on the walls. We had a new wooden floor laid in her room. It was a cosy little haven for her. But Robyn told me that Brian would sneak into her room at nightime and hide whatever dodgy item he had under the floorboards. She never knew what it was that he was hiding, as she was too afraid to look when she heard him coming. I can't imagine that she slept very soundly with that disturbance and the thought of something dodgy hidden under the floorboards.

Robyn and Joey had become very close, and over time

they became like sister and brother. They shared their thoughts, feelings and worries. Children should not have the kind of worries they had, but at least they had each other to confide in.

One time, while we were still living at Mitchelstown Cottage, Robyn became very ill. I took her to see the doctor, who told me that she was OK but had a fever. I brought her home and gave her some Nurofen, which the doctor had advised me to do. I still wasn't happy and could not see Robyn get any better as the night went on. She couldn't even keep water down. I slept on the sofa that night so that I could listen out for her. During the early hours of the morning, it must have been about five o'clock, Robyn woke me. She was standing in the doorway muttering my name. I took one look at her and immediately knew she was seriously ill. Her temperature was soaring, her skin looked a putty colour and she could barely move her head. I checked her body for a rash but couldn't find one, as I suspected it was meningitis. We quickly got dressed, jumped into the car and headed to Temple Street Hospital, where the doctors examined her and did some tests.

It was meningitis. Before bringing Robyn for a lumber puncture, the doctor showed me the rash that I couldn't find earlier. It was hidden between her toes. While she was been treated in hospital all of my family visited her, and Brian's family came to see her too. Brian visited her on one occasion, and Robyn recalls their conversation clearly. He told her that he was glad that she was in hospital and not at home. He said that he was happy now that we could be a real family, as she was gone and it was him, his girlfriend and their baby son at the cottage. I cannot imagine what she must have felt.

She hid a lot of things from me then, and it's too late for me to take them back now. I wish I knew what she was going through at the time.

ຍ ര

Young Joey spoke to Robyn about his feelings for Brian. Initially, he had trusted Brian and had thought of him as a father figure. When Joey moved into the house he hadn't seen Brian's violent side. When he eventually saw what Brian was capable of, it was too late for him to leave, because he was under Brian's control.

I learned that Joey wasn't doing too well on the witness protection programme. He was away from his family and friends, living abroad under a new identity. He felt very isolated and also had to leave his young daughter behind. It must have been a horrific time for him. I am sure that Joey is still haunted by his time at the cottage. All that I can say to him is: put it behind you and don't give it any more energy. Brian has taken enough of your strength. Joey has a lot to offer. He has a great sense of humour and a good heart. He is a trusting and loyal young man that gave up everything for justice.

Brian is serving time behind bars like a caged animal, and I can imagine how trapped he must be feeling. He loved his freedom. He was going to have to serve time with some of the inmates that he himself had probably helped to convict as a registered informant. Brian would soon feel the wrath of their vengeance. I believe that he has been attacked by other inmates.

During the trial, I left my job at Servisair. I could not stand the pressure from it all. I felt that I was losing my grip, and, again, I found myself hiding away. I must have been out of work for about five months or so before I eventually felt better. By then I had secured a permanent position with a company that handled business for a national airline. The Jonathan O'Reilly case had calmed down and I thought I was free of Brian.

I needed to get back to work to provide for my kids. Nearly a year had passed and I was enjoying my new job.

I was doing really well, working hard and getting on with my new colleagues.

Then, out of the blue, I received a phone call from the gardaí. They wanted to question me. I had no idea what for, as Brian was locked up. I thought, *this is never ending.*

When I got to the garda station, I was questioned about Brian and his garda friend. I couldn't tell them anything, because Brian had always kept their dealings under wraps. He never discussed their plans with me. He was very clever about that. All that I could tell them about was the events that I had actually witnessed. As far as I was aware, Brian usually met him in car parks or at venues around West Dublin.

The gardaí told me that there had been an investigation launched into a certain garda's alleged misconduct, and that the inquiry would hopefully clear his name. I spent three days with them, on and off, as they tried to piece together certain events that Brian had been involved in. I was so sick of all of this. When was it ever going to stop? I left the station feeling like I had been given my own life sentence because of my involvement with Kenny. Over those three days, I had to lie to yet another employer. I couldn't keep doing this. The past was holding onto me and I had to break free.

I kept on working and I heard no more from the

gardaí. But the panic attacks had returned, and I was feeling very down. I immediately assumed that every phone call or every knock at the front door would be related to Brian Kenny.

Chapter Ten

Putting the Past to Rights

When things had settled down somewhat, I decided to pursue my rights and stake my claim to the property in Kilshane. I still felt bitter and I was not happy to let Amanda Joyce have it so easily. I knew that Brian could no longer interfere or threaten me. I contacted Gerry Doherty, a solicitor in Finglas Village, who told me that he could pursue my claim. I often drove past the house in Kilshane. I was saddened to see that the cottage looked rundown. I know that I should have probably let it go, but that's easier said than done. The cottage was Conor's birthplace, so it was still dear to me in a strange sort of way.

One day a friend of mine told me to drive past the cottage as she thought something wasn't right. A family had been renting it for the previous few months. When I arrived at the cottage the windows seemed to be blacked out and one of them had wood covering it where the glass was missing. There were heavy chains on the gates at the front of the property. There was some garda forensic tape that was discoloured and seemed to have been there for some time. I parked the car and went to investigate.

I spoke to a neighbour and learned that the cottage had in fact gone up in flames. She pointed to a part of the roof that was missing. I was gobsmacked. She told me that the inside was gutted and that the cottage was now just a shell. I never found out what caused the fire. I don't know if it was started maliciously or by accident.

The property remains derelict to this day. When Brian was arrested, Amanda Joyce stayed on at the cottage, but only for a short time. I imagine she feared retaliation after Jonathan O'Reilly's murder. The house was then rented out so that the mortgage repayments could be met. I learned that Brian's mam had power of attorney and that she was looking after his interests.

On 11 March 2010 I attended Courtroom 28 in the Four Courts for the first hearing in relation to the property. Robyn accompanied me that day. I hadn't seen or spoken to the Kenny family for years and I was no longer afraid of them. They could try to intimidate us all they wanted. Robyn and I were stronger now.

When we arrived at Courtroom 28 I could see Billy

and Ann seated on one of the benches. Brian's grandmother was also present in a wheelchair. None of them looked our way, but Billy had obviously made Ann and the grandmother aware of our presence, as they remained seated with their backs to us. Robyn and I sniggered to one another.

My solicitor, Gerry Doherty, arrived and introduced me to my barrister, Bernadette Kirby. I was delighted that my barrister was a woman. I believed that she would fight tooth and nail for us. I caught a glimpse of Amanda Joyce through the crowds in the hall. Amanda had been called to the hearing as she was still married to Brian and obviously also had and interest in the cottage. I remember wondering how many more of the Kennys would arrive.

When Gerry Doherty and my barrister went into the courtroom to register the case, Robyn and I took our seats on the benches outside and waited to be called. Gerry returned and told us that they were waiting for Brian to arrive from Mountjoy Prison. On hearing this, Robyn and I laughed. I think we laughed because we couldn't believe it. I felt that the Kenny family was really trying their best to stop me getting my share of the property.

We were beginning to find the whole situation entertaining. Then I noticed Robyn's facial expression change to shock as she gestured for me to turn around and look behind me. Brian stood there in handcuffs, accompanied by two prison wardens. I looked him up and down and felt repulsed by him, so much so that I wanted to be sick.

Brian had aged and his skin had taken on a grey pallor. He looked terrified and paranoid. He looked at Robyn in disbelief, as she was now a young woman and not the vulnerable child that he remembered. The years had changed both of them in very different ways.

Eventually, we were called into court. The Kennys sat on the left-hand side and Robyn and I sat on the right side of the courtroom. Brian sat at the back of the court, still cuffed and flanked by the two officers.

The judge that day was also a woman. The hearing began and the judge heard from both sides. She tried to unravel the details, as things became more complicated when Amanda Joyce declared that she also had an interest in the property. When Brian's counsel introduced Amanda as Brian's wife, the judge asked her where her representation was. Amanda told the judge that she had none, as she had only been told about the hearing a couple of days before. It was now apparent that whatever the intention of bringing Amanda Joyce into the hearing had been, it was not going to plan – Amanda had her own ideas. At that point Ann Kenny wheeled her mother out of the courtroom, and it seemed to me that she was not too happy that Amanda was also looking for part of the property.

During the proceedings, a group of young schoolboys was brought into court and sat at the back of the room. I could hear them whisper and giggle amongst themselves. Amanda Joyce was standing in the middle of the courtroom, to Brian's left. When the judge asked her what the relationship between the two of them was now, Amanda answered:

'We don't live together now.'

'Obviously you don't live together now. You wouldn't be living where he is, would you?' said the judge.

The whole courtroom broke into laughter.

The judge that morning wasn't falling for anything Brian had instructed his barrister say. She was a tough lady. The hearing was eventually adjourned. Robyn told me that Brian couldn't take his eyes off us as he was led away.

When we left the courtroom Brian and the Kenny family seemed to have vanished. My barrister spoke to me outside. She was concerned because there was no paper trail to prove that I had lived at the cottage. Everything was in Brian's name, even down to the household bills. Brian had also lied and told them that I didn't move into the house when *he* had purchased it, but that I went to live there a year later. He was still trying his best to get one over on me. Even in his prison cell he was trying to wreck my head.

On 18 January 2011 my solicitor informed me that Brian's barrister had put proposals to settle the case. It was agreed that I would receive a percentage. However, my barrister worried that this would be a fraction of what I was entitled to. We went to the Law Library at 1.00 p.m. to hear the outcome. Again, Robyn came with me, and we joked on our way into town, wondering if it would turn into another circus performance.

When we got to the Law Library, Gerry and Bernadette were there to greet us. I noticed that this time Amanda Joyce had legal representation. The Kennys were nowhere to be seen. Brian's barrister was present to represent him, but his mam and dad were not. Robyn and I waited in a quiet hallway while the barristers went back and forth, trying to reach a settlement. As it turned out, nothing was settled that day.

My barrister told me that Ann Kenny had also engaged a solicitor to represent her, as she was now making a claim on the property herself. She was claiming that she had also put money into the cottage. Robyn and I were not surprised; we had expected their delay tactics. To me it seemed that she was trying to secure a larger portion for her son. I found it hard to understand this and I also felt that she was taking away from her grandson and what was rightfully his. I didn't care about percentages or money – I just wanted justice.

Another hearing date was set for 7 February 2011. Robyn and I arrived early at the Four Courts that day. Brian's solicitor had been hinting that they were willing to do a deal to reach a settlement. We hoped that that was the case and that we would finally be done with Brian and the Kennys.

When we arrived at Courtroom 28, Ann and Brian's sister were already there. Amanda Joyce was also present but she was not talking to the Kennys and a coolnesss appeared to have developed between them. Although Robyn and I suspected that this might have been staged in order to secure a larger portion of the estate for Brian, I was still quite entertained.

Brian was once again brought to court handcuffed and accompanied by prison wardens.

The case was put before the judge and he requested that all parties come to an agreement outside the courtroom.

We stood in the hallway for over an hour with the barristers shuffling back and forth, trying to reach some agreement that would satisfy everyone. My barrister was still worried about the lack of a paper trail linking me to Mitchelstown Cottage so I really wanted to get it sorted that day.

Amanda Joyce had told the court that she was applying for a separation order in the Family Court. This meant that our case could be dragged through the Family Court if we failed to reach a settlement that day. That would result in higher legal fees and the possibility of me ending up with nothing.

Eventually we agreed that I would receive 20 per cent of the property, Amanda Joyce would receive 20 per cent and Brian's parents would receive 20 per cent. Brian would be left with 40 per cent.

It's not the ideal outcome but I am happy with it and as Shakespeare said, I got 'my pound of flesh'.

The cottage will now be sold and the proceeds divided. A part of me feels sad about that. I loved that little cottage. But it brings the matter to a close and there is great relief in that too.

Chapter Eleven

Life Goes On

Violence of any type disgusts me and even more so when it is used on women. Why do so many men treat their wives or partners this way? I will never understand that. But why do women remain in the home? I do understand that. Women are afraid to leave, and they also try to keep their family unit together. As someone who has been in that position, I would say that you are no use to your children if you're not around to see them grow up.

But you also have to think of what your children witness and have to endure. Living in a home where there is a violent relationship shapes them for life. I held on to the relationship with Brian for as long as I could. I had two children with two different fathers, which is not something I am proud of, but I hoped that things would turn around. I was fooling myself. I was afraid to leave for fear of violent retaliation, and I was also afraid to find myself homeless. So for those reasons and those fears, I stayed for as long as I could. They might not seem reason enough to stay, but it seemed that way at the time. No matter which decision I made, I knew it wasn't going to be easy. I would have to make a sacrifice. I am glad that I choose to sacrifice the cottage and not my life.

When I think back to my time with Brian there were lots of external indicators that he was not liked. At the time I tried to ignore them and keep my head down in order to survive. I saw him in the company of some shady characters and witnessed the hatred that seemed to follow Brian around. He was crossing the wrong people without fearing the consequences.

I remember on a few occasions when we were out shopping together, coming across young men that would sneer and spit at him. These men called him a snitch, a rat and a liar. They were very hostile. I was always nervous when we came across them, though it didn't seem to bother Brian. I also remember being heckled. At the time, I had no idea what it was about, but I knew it had something to do with Brian. Some people who knew that we were a couple might have thought that I condoned or was involved in whatever it was Brian had done to them.

None of these people knew the truth behind our relationship. I was fighting my battle with Brian and I didn't need another one. Things were tough enough.

ꟷ ꟷ

Thankfully, we are all doing well today. Robyn is a successful young woman and I am very proud of her. She doesn't let anything get the better of her. She is ambitious and funloving and she is her mam's rock. Conor is now at secondary school. He is a typical young teenager: he loves his food and his Xbox 360. He's a funny, witty and easy-going young man with a very gentle way about him. I am a very proud mam. They kept me strong through all of the craziness.

I can only imagine what the outcome would have been if I had not left Mitchelstown Cottage with the kids. Brian would have moulded Conor, and God knows what he would have trained him to do.

Since leaving my job in October 2008, I have had a lot of time on my hands. I don't have the morning rush to work anymore, and I no longer have to care for my dear Mam.

Mam passed away in December of the same year.

After she died I felt that there was a huge void in my life. So I decided to write my account of events before somebody else decided to do it for me. I also wanted to write this for my children, so that they, especially Conor, would have some understanding of why we left Mitchelstown Cottage. I think that it is important that he understands when he is older. I am sure it will also cause Robyn to reflect. She remembers things that Conor is too young to remember. I hope that they will grow up having learned a lesson from our past and will never find themselves in a violent situation again.

ഇ ര

This is a different world from the one that our parents grew up in. Domestic violence was kept hidden back in those days – it is not today. Women are now stronger and are not afraid to speak out, but there are some that slip through the system and remain alone, dealing with this horrendous crime. Domestic violence can also affect men. They too can be recipients of violence and many men are too embarrassed and ashamed to speak out about their treatment. This shouldn't be the case. Abuse is abuse, in whatever form, and it needs to be exposed.

The present economic situation worries me for a number of reasons. Money problems have a big impact on families. As money is tight for a lot of people now, they feel under pressure to meet mortgage payments and pay bills. Some people worry about feeding their families on a budget, some remain sitting in the cold, afraid to turn the heating on. There are even those who are losing their homes. Anyone stuck in a violent situation will now worry even more about escaping. It might be the deciding factor in whether they feel able to make a break or not.

Most people are unaware of the new laws that the government is trying to introduce. If passed, this new law will allow anybody to report domestic abuse – it will not be up to the victim alone. A similar law was passed in Great Britain and Northern Ireland. We need to demand that the law is passed here. If you know of a case of violence against another person, report it and keep reporting it. Keep diaries if you can. It will help the victim in the event of a serious injury or if they eventually decide to report the perpetrator.

I was thirty when I met Brian Kenny, not a young girl starting out in life. I should have known better, but I really did not see it coming. I was nearly thirty-three when I gave birth to Conor, who is now thirteen. It is nearly nine years since I left Brian, but the ghosts are still following me around.

I would like to thank my parents for being my teachers and guides, and my sister Mary and brother Joe for being my crutches and advisors. They never judged me and I hope that they still see me as the same Rita – the Rita that plays guitar badly and drives them demented playing the tin whistle; the Rita that can't keep a secret and says all the wrong things at the wrong time, but never with malice; the Rita that never gives the mic back when the karaoke machine is on; the Rita that always got the blame for everything, even when she didn't do it – typical middle child syndrome.

I have come a long way since starting this book. It has been therapeutic for me, a kind of journey. I have looked over my shoulder and can now see the relationship that Brian Kenny and I had for what it was. I realise just how volatile it was. It was a scary and lonely place to be, and I will never allow myself to feel like that again. Writing this book is my way of moving on from the past and burying it for good.

It took me a long time before I felt that I could trust anyone again, especially a man. I was content to remain alone. I enjoyed the peace, the freedom and the independence that I had, but it was lonely too. The ordeal that

I endured living with Brian had left me hugely insecure. Although I enjoyed the company of my children and my mam, I eventually felt ready to move on with my life and share it with someone special again.

I am happy now. I am the happiest that I have been for a long, long time. I have shared the last five years of my life with a wonderful man named Tony Murray. I feel a connection with him that I have never felt with anyone else. He understands me. He supports me and he is proud of me. He is loving, caring and he has a kind soul. He makes me laugh and I feel that I have found my soulmate. It took me a long time, but I found him. He has made me strong and he has also made me believe in myself. I understand now just how strong a person I really am. Finishing this book has made me realise just how determined I am to leave the past behind, although I know that it will pop its head up every now and then, just to remind me of who I am: a true survivor.

The last few years have been wonderful. My life turned around and I have travelled a lot and seen some wonderful places that I thought I would never see. My life-long friends and family remain a solid presence in my life, and they are as brilliant as ever.

Tony is an amazing man and I hold him very close to my heart. I have never laughed as much as I have over the last few years since meeting him. We get on very well indeed. It was hard to trust anyone in the beginning, but I soon grew to love and trust him with anything – even my life. At first it was hard for Tony to fathom how Brian had treated me. He was shocked and horrified. He gets upset when he thinks of anyone ever hurting me. I know our love is true love. I had always considered myself damaged goods and I never thought that anyone would ever take me seriously again. How wrong was I?

Robyn and Conor have always remained loyal to their mam, even though I felt that I had let them down in the past. Robyn has convinced me that that was not the case. She says that she sees me as a strong woman who walked away and took them out of the hell that we were living in. She respects me more for having the courage to do that and then raise two children and work long hours so that they could have everything they needed. I have done my best. That's all any of us can do.

Tony proposed to me in the idyllic setting of Villeneuve Loubet, in Nice, on the French Riviera, and I accepted. We are looking forward to our future together.

My life has changed utterly and I am very, very happy. So are my children, and, as time passes, we are forgetting the past. Life is sweet again.

Epilogue

Raising Awareness

I hope that this book will help someone in some way. Maybe it will help to give the victims a voice. I believe that there should be a list, like the sex offenders list, so that those who prey on the vulnerable can be named and shamed. I know only too well how hard it is to report these crimes when you are living in fear, but that is what the victims have to find the courage to do. You may have been lucky enough to escape from a violent relationship, but you know that an abuser will move on to his next victim and that you must find your voice for them as much as for yourself.

Prehaps reading this book will help people gain an understanding of abusive relationships. I hope it helps increase awareness in our society, a society that generally doesn't tolerate such behaviour. Though we live in the twenty-first century, and women are more independent than ever before, there still needs to be more support and awareness of the difficulties the victims face and the fear they have to live with.

I have taken my life back and I am enjoying my freedom to live as I want to. I have no one to answer to but myself. The past has changed me. It has taught me to consider my decisions carefully, and not to jump in and repeat my mistakes. I take nothing for granted anymore, especially not the people that support me and that have helped me along the way.

I used to feel that I was fighting my battle with Brian alone. I didn't know which way to turn or what to do. When I eventually escaped from that life and told my family and friends about what I had endured, they were horrified. If you find yourself in the same situation, there are people out there who want to help you. All you have to do is ask. Name and shame your abuser and you will take away his power.

In a way we are all the makers of our own destiny. I moved on with my life and learned to trust again. It was not easy and in the beginning I thought that I was unworthy of having a normal life again. I no longer knew what my place in society was and I worried about what people thought of me. I had been stripped of any confidence and found it difficult to make decisions about anything. But I fought back with the help of my children, my family and my friends.

Appendix

Further Information

If you or someone you know has been affected by any of the issues raised in this book, please read the information below.

Domestic violence is the threat or use of physical, emotional, psychological and sexual abuse in close adult relationships. This includes destruction of property, isolation from family and friends or other potential sources of support and threats to others including children. Stalking and control over access to money, personal items, food, transport and the telephone are also common examples of domestic abuse. The overwhelming burden of partner violence is experienced by women. Domestic violence has severe and persistent effects on physical and mental health, and carries with it an enormous cost in terms of premature death and disability. If you are experiencing domestic violence there is help available. You will not be told what to do; you will be shown the options available to you. It's your life and your decision.

National Services:

Ambulance Service Tel: 999/112
Garda Síochána (24 hours) Tel: 999/112
or your local Garda Station
Rape Crisis Centre National Helpline (24 hours)
Tel: 1800 778888
Women's Aid Helpline (10am to 10pm) Tel: 1800 341900
AMEN Helpline for Men Who Experience Domestic
Abuse Tel: 046 90 23 718

Local Services for Women:

Information and support is available on many of the following areas: Domestic violence, rape and sexual assault, adult survivors of child abuse, crisis accommodation and refuges, empowerment and women's rights.

Source: http://www.socialwork.ie/socialwork/web-directory/crisis-services/domestic-violence services/rathmines-womens-refuge-dublin

Reproduced by kind permission of www.socialnetwork.ie